Active Learning Techniques for Librarians

CHANDOS
INFORMATION PROFESSIONAL SERIES

Series Editor: Ruth Rikowski
(email: Rikowskigr@aol.com)

Chandos'new series of books are aimed at the busy information professional. They have been specially commissioned to provide the reader with an authoritative view of current thinking. They are designed to provide easy-to-read and (most importantly) practical coverage of topics that are of interest to librarians and other information professionals. If you would like a full listing ofcurrent and forthcoming titles, please visit our web site www.chandospublishing.com or email info@chandospublishing.com or telephone +44(0) 1223 891358.

New authors: we are always pleased to receive ideas for new titles; if you would like to write a book for Chandos, please contact Dr Glyn Jones on email gjones@chandospublishing.com or telephone number +44 (0) 1993 848726.

Bulk orders: some organisations buy a number of copies of our books.If you are interested in doing this, we would be pleased to discuss a discount. Please email info@chandospublishing.com or telephone +44 (0) 1223 891358.

Active Learning Techniques for Librarians

Practical examples

ANDREW WALSH AND
PADMA INALA

Chandos Publishing
Oxford • Cambridge • New Delhi

Chandos Publishing
TBAC Business Centre
Avenue 4
Station Lane
Witney
Oxford OX28 4BN
UK
Tel: +44 (0) 1993 848726
Email: info@chandospublishing.com
www.chandospublishing.com

Chandos Publishing is an imprint of Woodhead Publishing Limited

Woodhead Publishing Limited
Abington Hall
Granta Park
Great Abington
Cambridge CB21 6AH
UK
www.woodheadpublishing.com

First published in 2010

ISBN:
978 1 84334 592 3

British Library Cataloguing-in-Publication Data.
A catalogue record for this book is available from the British Library.

Typeset by RefineCatch Limited, Bungay, Suffolk
Printed in the UK and USA.

To Jenny and George who make their Daddy smile every day.
To Mum, Nana and the Dias family.

Contents

Acknowledgements

Many thanks to Emily Shields and Rosie Jones at Manchester Metropolitan University for inspiring us both in their work and talks at LILAC; for patiently correcting many of our errors when writing this book; and also for all their helpful advice and suggestions. Also thanks to Sarah, Ellie and Deborah at the University of Huddersfield for reading the draft and providing many suggestions for improvements.

About the authors

Andrew Walsh is an Academic Librarian at the University of Huddersfield, West Yorkshire, UK and has worked in most of the subject teams, but is currently looking after the Schools of Education and Professional Development and Music, Humanities and Media. He has been a Chartered Librarian for several years, is a member of the Higher Education Academy, and has worked in academic libraries since gaining his MSc. He is particularly interested in the field of information literacy, including improving further the standard of teaching skills within his library service and the wider professional community, which includes the use of active learning techniques within library sessions. Actively engaged with the use of mobile and Web 2.0 technologies in the library environment, he has encouraged the appropriate use of Twitter, blogs, social networking tools, text messaging (SMS) and mobile friendly materials to support users. As part of this work, he won the UC&R (University, College and Research) Group Innovation Award 2009 for a project pioneering the use of mobile phone friendly information skills materials. Another interest is the potential impact of the library on student achievement, and he is researching the links between library involvement in information skills instruction, library usage and final grades achieved by students. He is also studying part time for a PhD, investigating the perceptions of law staff and students towards information literacy. He regularly gives talks on subjects including information literacy, active learning and mobile learning within libraries. He has also written journal articles on a range of topics, listed on *http://eprints.hud.ac.uk/view/authors/Walsh=3AAndrew=3A=3A.html* together with selected conference papers.

Padma Inala is a Senior Assistant Librarian at Manchester Metropolitan University, Manchester, UK. She is a chartered librarian and has over ten years' experience of working within libraries in both the commercial and academic environment. She is currently a subject librarian for the Institute of Education, where she teaches information skills to all levels of students, from foundation courses through to masters and doctorate level. After investigating information literacy teaching for her MSc dissertation, a career-long interest in IL was fostered. On returning to HE librarianship she became interested in how students' learning of information literacy can be increased with the use of interactive teaching methods. She furthered this interest by completing a qualification in training and learning, and in her role at MMU's Didsbury campus library she was involved in a 2008/9 university-wide project looking at the role audience response systems can play in student learning and assessment. Although voting systems and their part in IL training are Padma's main interest, she is also keen to explore and experiment with lo-tech ways of engaging with her audience. As she teaches a range of group sizes from a number of academic levels in a variety of environments, she is ideally placed to have experimented with many of the activities in this book. The authors may be contacted via the publishers.

What is active learning?

Introduction

There is no doubt that in recent years the role of the librarian has changed. There are a number of factors that have contributed to this transformation, but it is the numerous technological advances and the rapidly changing information landscape that have caused the most significant changes to our profession (Dodd, 2007). The publication, storage and retrieval of information has altered dramatically in the last 15 years and now relies heavily on the use of technology and technological equipment to manage and access this information.

As librarians we need to keep up-to-date with these advances and be able to show an understanding and knowledge of these new information mechanisms and technologies, not only to move the service forward but also to enable us to meet the information needs of our users. As a result, librarians are increasingly expected to do more than simply just show individual users how to use these new technologies; many are now expected to teach groups of users how to interact, manipulate and fully exploit these various new resources to find information (Dodd, 2007).

Much of this is done by librarians who have not had any previous teaching experience or have not undertaken any type of formal teaching qualifications. Some may get basic in-house training, or even just get to shadow a more experienced member of staff, but rarely are they sent on formal, external courses. These courses would address the basic principles of teaching and learning, such as educational theories or methods, or other important practical issues such as designing, planning and delivering teaching sessions. Yet, librarians are increasingly being asked to run sessions and teach groups of users as part of their day-to-day duties without this knowledge or training. Furthermore, the majority of teaching in libraries is often done in 'one-off' teaching sessions, rather than in weekly or monthly sessions where there is regular contact with learners. Seeing learners regularly tends to be more synonymous with traditional teaching, where knowledge, understanding and learning are built up gradually and assessed over a period of time. The majority of librarians, however, have only this one-off session to ensure that an individual has not only grasped the new skill or concept but also gained sufficient knowledge to feel competent or be able to replicate it independently when needed at a later date.

While librarians and library staff have always had to instruct users how to use a certain number of resources such as catalogues and bibliographic databases and had to show them how to search the shelves, running structured teaching sessions to groups presents a number of challenges and many librarians and library staff are left feeling ill-equipped and daunted by the prospect of running such sessions. These challenges are being faced not only by existing library staff who have found themselves having to adapt to this new role but also by newly employed library staff who may have never embarked upon any type of instruction or teaching before.

Some of the main challenges to library staff are planning, creating and delivering sessions that can hold the attention of the users. In the past, it has been noted by many that library inductions (and orientation) and library instruction have elicited more than a few yawns from users on numerous occasions. The view from the users' perspective is that these sessions will be boring, uninteresting and unengaging, and therefore little is gained from them (Todd, 2006). As more and more information becomes available through a variety of mediums and technologies, it is important that we are at the forefront in teaching and showing users how to exploit these resources. It is therefore more crucial than ever that we are able to deliver engaging and participative sessions that enhance knowledge and skills.

This book explores the use of a number of active learning techniques within the context of library instruction and teaching, primarily where librarians and library workers are required to teach one-off sessions.

The authors understand that this role as teachers as well as the type of sessions delivered by librarians at their individual organisations will vary greatly – not only in content, delivery and context but also in expectation of the type of results they want to achieve depending on their library sector. Given this diversity in roles, the activities in this book are designed to be adapted and modified to suit the needs of the relevant sector that is being taught.

Many of the activities and techniques presented in the book have largely been used by the authors not only in libraries within a higher education setting but also at some conferences and presentations to other librarians and library staff.

It is a practical resource to be dipped in and out of when needed and aims to appeal to a wide readership within the profession, particularly where teaching is a key part of the role. This includes graduate trainees and also students of librarianship and/or information studies.

The book is split into three chapters:

The first chapter briefly outlines the theory and practice of active learning, what active learning is, the benefits and advantages of using active learning techniques, and finally the importance of using active learning techniques within a library setting.

The second chapter is the largest section of the book and provides a number of practical activities and tips to help you establish active learning techniques in your library sessions. There are five sections of 'interactive nuggets' in this chapter, split into categories, beginning with techniques to help with *Starting and finishing the session*. This is followed by *In the middle*, which provides general tips and activities that can be used at any time and at any point during teaching sessions. The next two sections contain activities and tips specifically for running sessions using *Mobile phones and other gadgets* in your sessions and using *Web 2.0 technologies*. The final section in this chapter has activities that are dedicated to running *Inductions*.

Each tip or activity includes the following information to help you with your planning:

■ Uses

■ Materials required

■ Notes

■ How to use it

■ Variations

■ Pitfalls

The third chapter contains sample lesson plans as examples of how active learning tips may be used in a complete lesson. They can be used straight out of the book, amended to your own needs or as templates for creating your own. The detailed plans contain all the information you will need to plan and run a one-hour library teaching session.

Each plan contains the following information:

■ Techniques used from this book

■ Target audience

■ Maximum class size

- Expected outcomes
- Time
- Handouts required
- Equipment required
- Outline of session (including suggested timings)

What is active learning?

The term active learning has been widely used in the education and teaching world for a number of years and is considered as a constructivist approach to learning (Pritchard, 2008). This approach seeks to involve students in their own learning and for them to actively take part in the learning process themselves, rather than being simply fed information (Chickering and Gamson, 1987; Pritchard, 2007). It is an approach that sees the importance and relevance in their experience and in understanding how the learner arrives at the outcome, not just the outcome itself.

More recently, active learning has transcended beyond just traditional educational circles and is now a method of learning widely used in various types of teaching, training and instruction in a variety of environments and sectors – public, private and commercial.

There are numerous definitions and anecdotal descriptions of the term, but active learning is most commonly described as 'learning by doing' (Gibbs, 1988). The basic principle lies in the theory that people learn more and are more likely to retain that information if they are actively engaged in the learning process. In other words, by being involved in the learning through doing, discussing, questioning and applying, there is more emphasis on learners working it out for themselves and developing a better understanding than if they were just given the information. This then transfers into the knowledge they will need to undertake the task or activity independently at another time.

In order to achieve this, active learning also requires people to draw upon and use their existing knowledge, skills and experiences, to aid their new learning. In doing so it will make learning a more fluid, involved process that encourages participation rather than a one-way process in which students rely on teachers to give them information and facts (Lorenzen, 2001). There are various other approaches to learning such as collaborative, cooperative, problem-based and student centred learning, all of which use activity and interaction as the key to learning and are considered by many as a subset of active learning (Chalmers, 2008).

Delivering lectures has traditionally been a popular method of teaching and is still used in a variety of courses and lessons, including library instruction, but it does not provide learners with many opportunities to engage or interact in the learning processes themselves. Most commonly, the teacher stands at the front and does all the talking, thinking and questioning. It has been argued (Bonwell and Eison, 1991) that lecturing provides very little scope for reflection or analysis of the material being taught as students are often either fed information from the teacher or just given handouts that consequently do not help to develop thinking and writing skills. Many learners therefore either do not bother to listen or find themselves in a situation where they can barely make clear, coherent notes from what is being taught, let alone be able to think and reflect upon it.

Lectures also require the undivided attention of the learner, which in many cases means listening and concentrating solely on the speaker for anything up to 40 minutes or longer. A study by Meyers and Jones (1993) revealed that students are most attentive in the first ten minutes of a lecture, but this attention then drops dramatically and stays low until the last five or ten minutes before the end of the lecture. Students therefore are unable to fully absorb or process the necessary information presented to them in order to have a full learning experience. Other studies (Middendorf and Kalish, 1996) conclude similar findings that put the attention span of an average adult at anywhere between six and 20 minutes, although it was noted that this can vary owing to other factors such as the time of day, the heat of the room, the tiredness of the learner. The lecture style of teaching makes it almost impossible for a student to reach their optimal learning level.

In contrast to such passive learning techniques, active learning is about creating an environment where students can take charge of their learning, see relevance in it and engage in it, instead of having information just delivered to them.

Strategies that promote active learning are said to have a number of common characteristics:

- Students are involved in more than just listening.
- Less emphasis is placed on transmitting information and more on developing students' skills.
- Students are involved in higher order thinking (analysis, synthesis and evaluation)
- Students are engaged in activities (e.g. reading, discussing and writing).
- Greater expectation is placed on the students' exploration of their attitudes and values.

(Bonwell and Eison, 1991)

Active learning techniques that can be used in teaching can include discussion, games, debate, role-play exercises, group work, case studies and peer teaching (Jensen, 2005). These all help the learner interact and engage with other learners of different abilities and who have different experiences and knowledge.

By employing and encouraging active learning techniques and strategies, learners are able to become much more involved and can take more responsibility for their own learning. The teacher therefore is no longer seen as the expert who has all the answers and the sole keeper of all the knowledge (Breslow, 1999) but serves more as a facilitator or coach to help learners realise their own potential and find solutions and answers by using their existing skills and those of others in the group to develop and learn. This in turn will help them develop analytical skills and critical thinking and encourages independent learning (Bonwell and Eison, 1991). This is an important aspect of using active learning techniques, particularly in a library environment where learners are more likely to attend just one session and may not have the opportunity to attend another session at a later date. Therefore, they will need to gain as much knowledge and/or skills as possible in a short time so that they will be able to apply this knowledge in future, probably without assistance.

Another significant aspect of using active learning techniques over passive ones is that it creates the opportunity and the ability for the teacher to provide timely feedback. With active learning, feedback can be incorporated into the activity and can be given at a point where learners are able to reassess or revaluate and perhaps correct any mistakes and change their mind or their behaviour (Chickering and Gamson, 1987; Jensen, 2005). For example, activities that involve voting or sharing answers enable the teacher to find out much more quickly what the learner knows and doesn't know. The teacher can then either recap or adapt the session to ensure that there is understanding, so that the learner gains the correct knowledge. What is most important here is that the learner is given the opportunity to check whether learning has taken place, whereas with many passive learning techniques these opportunities simply do not exist and learners leave thinking that they have understood something, when in fact they may not have.

While active learning aims to engage the participants and encourage interactivity as an aid to learning and teaching, it is also useful in addressing the different learning capabilities and styles of the class. It has been well documented that individuals learn in different ways, each person having a set of strengths and weaknesses in the way he or she learns and processes information (Meyers and Jones, 1993; Honey and Mumford 2000). Gardner's (1983) research on multiple intelligences proposed that all individuals can be intelligent in different ways, not just in the traditional academic sense in which intelligence is normally defined but that people have other kinds of intelligences with which they are just as capable of learning and excelling. For example, learners may have high spatial intelligence with which they can relate and transfer information in picture or image form and learn visually. Others may have high kinaesthetic intelligence with which they can transfer and understand information better if they can handle and feel objects. Each learner is therefore different in the way in which he or she can take in and understand information. Active learning provides the platform on which to address some of these issues and allows for the teacher to provide learning that can cater to these needs.

There are also a number of other theories that are based on the idea that each person has a preferred way of learning – a style of learning to which he or she is more suited – by which he or she is more likely to take in new knowledge or skills. By catering to that preferred style, the learner will be more open to receiving and processing information as the information is presented in a way that is compatible with his or her learning and understanding. One example is Honey and Mumford's (2000) learning styles research, based on the four stages of Kolb's (1984) learning cycle: having an experience (the activist stage), reviewing the experience (the reflector stage), concluding from the experience (the theorist stage) and planning the next steps (the pragmatist stage). They believed that all four stages of the cycle are necessary for effective learning, but that most people develop a preference for a particular stage, and get caught in the cycle, making that stage and style more dominant in their learning (Honey and Mumford, 2000). The four learning styles they identified are as follows.

- *Activists* – who tend to want to get stuck into things straight away and be engaged in doing things. They like to learn by participating rather than listening for long periods of time.
- *Reflectors* – who tend to prefer to sit back, listen and observe before they take any action. They like to learn by researching and being prepared.
- *Theorists* – who tend to be logical, rational and objective. They like to know the facts and be able to analyse them before acting.
- *Pragmatists* – who tend to make practical decisions, solve problems and get on with things. They like to try out new things only if they can see how they can be applied in practice.

Honey and Mumford devised a lengthy questionnaire in which each person receives a final score for each of the four styles. Everyone will have an element of each of these styles, but the styles with higher scores indicate the preference to which each individual is best suited. This diversity in learning styles means that each individual learner will take in and process information differently and his or her ability to learn can often be determined by the way in which the teaching session is delivered.

Active learning helps to tackle some of these issues as it is highly unlikely that when teaching any sized group, collectively the whole group will share the same preference for learning. In such groups, most individuals will not have undertaken any type of learning analysis and therefore may not be aware of their own preferred learning style, but active learning can enable you to address a variety of learning styles within a teaching session. By selecting certain tasks and alternating and introducing different activities you can cater for, and play to, the strengths of all learners.

Don't be misled into thinking that all active learning must involve high-energy, physical tasks. Active learning can be reading something, then reflecting and reporting on it or having to work something out or problem solve. The key to remember is that it requires the learner to think and question and to interact with, or react to, the learning materials, rather than just read notes or be lectured at.

Importance of active learning in library teaching

Librarians who teach often end up using the same techniques and styles time and time again, even when these may not work as effectively as they could. Some of this is down to the fact that most have probably not received any training in how to plan or write sessions and this can seem daunting. Some of it may also be down to the ease and convenience of using something that is already prepared as writing, planning and designing sessions takes time, and many librarians might not always have time available. For us to be able to encourage learning and understanding, we as librarians need to look for new ways to teach and new ways in which to effectively engage learners, make the sessions fresh and interesting and to encourage learners to see the importance and relevance in library instruction.

Most forms of library induction or teaching have traditionally been in the form of a lecture-style session where the librarian gives a presentation either followed by or interspersed with a demonstration of the relevant resources. Even though interspersing the session with a demonstration is a form of interactivity, the learners still do not get the opportunity to try out the task themselves, they can still only watch and take notes. The learners do not fully engage with either the resource or other learners.

Many librarians may already be using some form of active learning in their teaching such as asking for a show of hands or passing library materials around, but how many of us have delivered sessions only to be stared back at with blank faces or learners who look uninterested?

As discussed in the previous section, lectures do not always provide the right environment for most individuals to take control of their learning or for them to be able to reach their potential learning ability. Gibbs' study of higher education in the 1990s showed that students who had the highest levels of achievement had all attended courses where active learning was used and where there was interaction with others (Petty, 2004). In a similar study where learners' knowledge and achievements have been measured, there was a notable increase in either marks or outcome when active learning was used (Breslow, 1999).

Librarians typically teach in one-off sessions because the information and skills taught tend not to follow any curriculum or formal assessment. This kind of teaching differs from that of traditional teachers, in which they regularly see their class and can build knowledge and skills over a period of time. In this situation the teacher can pick up and address any learning issues or problems the learner may be having in understanding what is being taught some days or weeks afterwards or after an assignment or examination. However, by only seeing the learner once and for a relatively short time, providing this longer, ongoing learning relationship is not possible.

As a consequence our library teaching needs to be focused, meaningful and participative as learners' successes or weaknesses need to be addressed within the session in order to achieve any learning outcomes (Jensen, 2005). The use of active learning can help to address some of these issues.

The use of active learning is important for library teaching as it is learner centred; it encourages participation and the ability of the learner to engage with learning materials and/or other learners. During a traditional lecture-style library session, we probably spend the majority of the time speaking, presenting information and demonstrating and answering questions. The learners often remain passive, just listening and perhaps writing, but they do not have the opportunity to actively participate in their learning. The lesson can sometimes become dominated by us and by the presentation; whereas if learners are given the opportunity to become involved through activity, the focus of the session then becomes all about them. For example, getting the group to work in pairs or small groups to work out a problem and asking them to write their feedback on the board, or give verbal feedback to the whole group, makes the learners not only engage with their peers but also draw upon and use existing knowledge or skills in order to carry out the activity.

We should not spend the majority of the lesson just demonstrating a database or a catalogue, expecting learners to have understood, but should allow them the time to put the information into practice. Set your group an activity so that they can use it for themselves, let them make mistakes and then let them try to find their own solutions, before giving them the answers or doing it for them. Using active learning helps shift some of the focus away from the teacher and onto the learner, encouraging learners to think more, apply existing knowledge, and take more responsibility for their own learning and development. A lot of library instruction can be very task based, but when we are teaching we should not only be interested in gaining an end result, we need to focus on the experience the learner will have. If this journey is one where interactivity and stimulation takes place, in an environment that encourages thinking, doing, discussing and reflecting then there is more likelihood that the information will be retained and there will be some sense of understanding of the process, and therefore the learner will be enabled to independently replicate what has been learnt. This process that an individual goes through to achieve new knowledge or skills is one in which the learning takes place (Pritchard, 2008). It is important for us as librarians to empower learners to use this knowledge and if we encourage good learning techniques then users become self-reliant.

One of the most important aspects of active learning in library teaching is that it facilitates both assessment and feedback, both of which can help to focus on the learners' needs. In most library sectors, librarians run teaching sessions where no formal assignment or assessment is required at the end – it can sometimes be hard to incorporate and more often can be overlooked. However, the instruction, training and information provided in these sessions is an essential support to other functions of the wider organisation or service, e.g. school, university, legal firm, hospital, etc. In his research on school librarians and student learning in Ohio, Todd (2006: 36) found that the school librarian role was one that was both 'active and learning centred' and that their role as information experts was essential in working alongside teachers to help students understand how to use and process information effectively to gain knowledge and skills.

By using more practical activities, tasks or problem solving, it enables librarians to assess the level of knowledge and learning at the point of the activity. This in turn provides the opportunity for the librarian to address this and give appropriate feedback or further instruction at the time when it is most useful to the learner, rather than after the session has finished or giving none at all.

Many traditional library sessions that rely on just a lecture or presentation do not allow for this kind of assessment or feedback by librarians, nor do they allow the learners the opportunity to realise they have misunderstood, or not understood at all. They may well leave the session thinking they have a grasp on what was taught, but in reality, they have not and therefore when they try to replicate what was taught, they are unable to. In this instance, learners have not had a positive learning experience, they have not gained new skills or knowledge and it is unlikely they will have the chance to attend another session to rectify this. Also, feedback alone does not always allow learners to know exactly what they have done. Sometimes learners might think that they haven't grasped what was being taught, when in fact, they have understood it quite well. Practical activities, assessment and feedback all allow for these issues to be addressed.

While most active learning assessment techniques in library teaching are very informal, such as show of hands, voting cards, audience response voting pads, questionnaires or quizzes etc., they nonetheless provide librarians with the opportunity to provide feedback to the learner there and then at the point of need, where it can be related and corrected accordingly, both of which are important factors in the learning process. For example, in their pilot project using audience response voting pads to teach information literacy sessions to university students, Jones et al. (2007) used the pads – in anonymous mode – to conduct a knowledge check at the start of their session to see how confident the students felt in using library resources. This assessment is twofold as it provided them with information regarding the students' current level of knowledge as well as allowing the students the opportunity to disclose their feelings towards using library resources. Even though this is a relatively minor form of assessment, it still provides the teacher with some vital information from which, if needed, he or she can adapt the session to incorporate either more advanced techniques or simpler ones, depending on the results.

Designing and planning lessons around what the learner needs to know is an important aspect of teaching any session and ensuring that there are clear objectives means that learners have some idea of what they can expect to learn and should have learnt by the end of the session. But active learning provides the platform for librarians to use assessment and feedback more effectively, making sure that the objectives of the lesson are met, by focusing on the needs of the learner.

In addressing the need to provide a more focused, relevant and meaningful teaching session we must also take into account the different learning styles and learning intelligences of the class. Active learning, as we explained earlier, helps accommodate different learning styles by enabling one to incorporate a variety of activities into the session that will not only appeal to, but also benefit different types of learners. Providing some variety and alternatives to the bog standard presentation and handouts, which may only appeal to the visual learners or reflectors in the room, will make the session more engaging for all learners and hopefully gain their interest and enable them to process and retain the information presented more effectively (Bellanca, 1997).

With the recent rise in technological inventions and advancements, active learning also facilitates the use of a variety of technological equipment and technology. Many young users are technology savvy, they are used to using a multitude of electronic gadgets in their daily lives, have grown up surrounded by them and conduct the majority of their studies, work and social lives through them. If budget allows incorporating active learning techniques through the use of equipment such as mobile phones and handheld gaming units, one can capture the attention and increase interest within a group. Also, utilising the new technological gadgets, the internet and its wealth of resources, particularly Web 2.0 technology, in which users can interact, through social networking sites (e.g. Facebook, Twitter, Flickr, etc.), blogs, podcasts, wikis, and video- and audio-conferencing and RSS feeds, can be a way of stimulating interaction and increased enthusiasm, motivation and interest in the activities (Gooding, 2008). Using these technologies for teaching might be a new and daunting area for many librarians, but they may engage learners more fully in ways that traditional activities are unable to. We are aware that this is a new area for many and so have addressed tips for using these technologies in the second chapter of the book under two separate sections titled 'Mobile phones and other gadgets' and 'Web 2.0' technologies.

While it is nice to have flashy gadgets and technology, the environment or budget does not need to be a barrier to active learning (Jones et al., 2007). Active learning encompasses 'learning by doing' and interactivity; it does not necessarily need lots of money to fund it – using simple methods such as coloured card for voting, or paper or online quizzes and questionnaires, or using simple props that you may already have will suffice. Even with none at all you can be creative with the space you have. It is about engaging learners, making them think and interact in the learning process. The majority of the activities in both *Starting and finishing the session* and *In the middle* contain a variety that do not need much equipment, money or resources to implement.

We need to provide interesting, engaging sessions that employ active learning techniques and encourage learners to think, question and apply their knowledge to situations and activities in order to gain a greater understanding of what is being taught and for them to gain the new knowledge they require. It is important for us to ensure that our learners achieve this, as in many libraries, one-off sessions are taught and it may be a learner's one and only chance to attend. Therefore, for us as librarians to be able to provide the maximum learning experience, we need to think about moving away from static lectures and presentations, and adopt a more fluid, two-way strategy for teaching.

References

Bellanca, J. (1997) *Active Learning Handbook for the Multiple Intelligences Classroom.* Arlington Heights, IL: IRI/Skylight Training and Publishing.
Bonwell, C.C. and Eison, J.A. (1991) *Active Learning: Creating Excitement in the Classroom.* ASHE-Eric Higher Education Report No. 1. Washington, DC: The George Washington University, School of Education and Hunan Development.

Breslow, L. (1999) *New Research Points to the Importance of Using Active Learning in the Classroom.* Teach Talk, MIT Faculty Newsletter Vol. XIII, No. 1, September/October. 6 January 2010. Online at: *http://web.mit.edu/tll/ tll-library/teach-talk/new-research.html.*

Chalmers, M. (2008) 'Lessons from the academy: actuating active mass-class information literacy instruction', *Reference Services Review*, 36 (1): 23–38.

Chickering, A.W. and Gamson, Z.F. (1987) *Seven Principles for Good Practice in Undergraduate Education*, 23 August 2009. Online at: *http://honolulu.hawaii. edu/intranet/committees/FacDevCom/guidebk/teachtip/7princip.htm.*

Dodd, L. (2007) 'The future of librarianship: moving out of the library and into the faculty. How problem based learning is transforming the traditional role', *SCONUL Focus*, 41 (Summer/Autumn): 4–8.

Gardner, H. (1983) *Frames of Mind: The Theory of Multiple Intelligences.* New York: Basic Books.

Gibbs, G. (1988) *Learning by Doing: A Guide to Teaching and Learning Methods.* London: Further Education Unit.

Gooding, J. (2008) 'Web 2.0: a vehicle for transforming education', *International Journal of Information and Communication Technology Education*, 4 (2): 44–53.

Honey, P. and Mumford, A. (2000) *The Learning Styles Helper's Guide.* Maidenhead: Peter Honey Publications.

Jones, R., Peters, K. and Shields, E. (2007) 'Transform your training: practical approaches to interactive information literacy teaching', *Journal of Information Literacy*, 1 (1): 35–42.

Jensen, E. (2005) *Teaching with the Brain in Mind*, revised 2nd edn. Alexandria, VA: Association for Supervision and Curriculum Development.

Kolb, D. (1984) *Experiential Learning.* Englewood Cliffs, NJ: Prentice Hall.

Lorenzen, M. (2001) *Active Learning and Library Instruction.* 9 September 2009. Online at: *http://www.libraryinstruction.com/active.html.*

Meyers, C. and Jones, T.B. (1993) *Promoting Active Learning: Strategies for the College Classroom.* San Francisco: Jossey-Bass.

Middendorf, J. and Kalish, A. (1996) 'The "Change-up" in lectures', *The National Teaching and Learning Forum*, 5 (2). 23 August 2009. Online at: *http://www.ntlf.com/html/pi/9601/article1.htm.*

Petty, G. (2004) *Active Learning Works: The Evidence.* 9 September 2009. Online at: *http://www.geoffpetty.com/downloads/WORD/ActiveLearningWorks.doc*

Pritchard, A. (2007) *Effective Teaching with Internet Technologies: Pedagogy and Practice.* London: Paul Chapman.

Pritchard, A. (2008) *Ways of Learning: Learning Theories and Learning Styles in the Classroom*, 2nd edn. Abingdon, Oxon: David Fulton.

Todd, R. (2006) 'It's all about getting A's', *Update*, 5 (1–2): 34–6.

2

Active learning tips

Starting and finishing the session

This chapter covers the activities that could easily be dropped into the start or end of many teaching sessions. You might think it strange that we've grouped opposite ends of a lesson into one chapter – surely they're completely different? No, in fact many sorts of activities that you may wish to use at these opposite ends of your lesson have many similarities and most of our examples would work well in both these places.

At the start of any class, it is good practice to take some sort of snapshot of knowledge and expectations so that you know what needs to be covered in the time you have. Without this you risk your whole lesson wasting your own and learners' time. How can you teach a subject if you don't know where your class is starting from? It is also a good practice to set up the expectations of the class right from the start. If they know within the first few minutes of a lesson starting that you will be expecting their active engagement, it will set the tone of the whole lesson, easing them into the rest of the activities you have planned, and pulling them together so that there is a group understanding of what you expect from the class. There are many icebreakers you may be able to use to set up these expectations, but instead of including pure 'icebreakers', we've tried to make sure they all have a primary function, with that of icebreaker normally being a bonus.

Equally, by the end of the class, you need to be sure that the topics you have been teaching have been understood. Again, everyone's time will have been wasted if no learning has taken place, and as librarians we typically have very little teaching time and cannot afford to waste it! You should also end your lesson knowing your class have a clear idea of how they will apply the knowledge gained in that session.

The start and end of a teaching session therefore both need ways of checking knowledge and should be an opportunity to bring the class together to form a clear idea of expectations. Preferably in our normally very limited contact time, in ways that are quick and easy to carry out!

As such, this chapter provides ways of easily checking knowledge, setting up the expectation of active involvement in their learning, and helping your learners express how they will develop and apply the knowledge and skills gained in their future work and study.

All stand

Uses: A quick test of knowledge that can be competitive if you wish.

Materials required: None.

Notes: Very easy and quick method that can be used in any session, whatever be the size.

How to use it:

- Ask the whole class to stand up.
- Ask the class a question with two possible answers, preferably with YES/NO or TRUE/FALSE answer. Tell them to stay standing for one response and to sit for the other.
- Ask another question, but only those who got the first one correct take part.
- Continue as long as you want!

Variations: Use for Boolean search terms – those people who satisfy the search you call out stay standing, the others sit down, similar to 'Guess Who?', the board game, but with Boolean operators thrown in! So, for instance, you could tell them to stay standing if they are 'Male AND wear glasses'.

Pitfalls: Some people may be uncomfortable standing up, feeling that they are 'on display' in some way. Keep an eye out for signs of discomfort in your class, and use more anonymous ways of testing knowledge if you need to.

Any improvements?

Uses: A way of checking improvements in knowledge between the start and end of a class, to make students realise that they have learnt something! Helps you fine tune your session depending on how knowledgeable they feel they are at the start.

Materials required: A small (A5 or A6) piece of card for each student.

Notes: This is a very quick test of knowledge or perceived skill at the start and end of a session.

How to use it:

- Distribute a card to each student.
- Ask them to write down how much they know about a topic, how long they spend carrying out a task, or how confident they feel carrying out a task.
- Collect the responses together at the front of the class.
- Collate the responses in a way you can easily read or display to the class.
- At the end of a session, ask the same question again and once more collate the responses – you may have to do this verbally or as a show of hands to save time collating the responses.
- Hopefully you'll be able to show an improvement between the start and end of the session.

Variations: Use interactive handsets (clickers) for instant responses to your question – remember to save the responses from the start, however, or you won't be able to carry out the comparison.

Pitfalls: If there is no real improvement, it can be really embarrassing!

Bag of fears

Uses: This can be a nice way to acknowledge students' fears about a topic and to reassure the members of your class that it is okay that they don't know everything.

Materials required: Small piece of card for each student (A5 or A6).

Notes: Make sure you allow enough time to cover all the fears at the end of the session – you may not have covered all the fears in the main session. It helps if you can scan through them part way through the session, perhaps during an activity or discussion, so you can adapt the session accordingly.

How to use it:

- Distribute a card to each student.
- Ask them to write down the biggest fear about the topic you are about to cover.
- Collect the responses together in a bag or opaque wallet.
- At the end of a session review each 'fear' and ask if it has been addressed.

Variations: With a large group, or if you are worried you may not have time to sort through the cards, you could ask the class themselves to partially sort through the cards for you. Ask them to write their own list, or as a pair. Then compile them together as a group of four, possibly scaling up to eight (two groups combined) and sixteen, if the layout of the room allows them to work together in this way.

Pitfalls: If you don't manage to sort through the 'fears' and address them during the session, the members of the class with those concerns may feel more frustrated than if you hadn't asked for their 'fears' in the first place. Make sure you build in enough flexibility to address everything that may come up, even if it is just to say you will provide more support or information afterwards.

Class concerns

Uses: Focuses attention on the session at hand. Highlight common experiences, anxieties, and expectations. Allows you to adjust your teaching according to the concerns of the class.

Materials required: Small piece of card for each student (A5 or A6).

Notes: This is a non-threatening way of gathering consensus from the class as to what material should be covered in the session. It works in both large and small groups, though in a large lecture theatre you will need to make it clear that when the cards reach the end of a row, they should be passed on to the row in front. You'll also need an assistant to shuttle cards from the front to the back of the class, and collect them some time into the session once the cards have had a chance to circulate through the whole room.

How to use it:

- Distribute a card to each student.
- Ask them to write down the main thing they'd like to learn from the session or any concerns they have about the subject you'll be covering.
- Get the students to pass the card to the person immediately to their right.
- Ask them to read their neighbour's card and tick the card if they also would like that question asked.
- Repeat until the cards reach the original writers of the questions.
- Identify which questions received the most votes (ticks) and either answer them immediately, explain they will be answered later, or explain why you won't be covering that material and perhaps point them in the direction of further help to cover the question.
- Collect all the cards in and look at them at a later date to check what sort of questions or concerns the students have.

Variations: A simpler method, that won't collect the same richness of suggestions from the class, is to ask the class to call out the main things they'd like to see covered in the session (one row at a time in large lecture theatres). Then take a show of hands to vote on the most popular questions or topics.

Pitfalls: It can take a while to pass the cards around the class, especially if you are in a large room!

Closing circle

Uses: Gives you an idea of what students have found useful in a session and reminds students what you've covered in the session. Encourages reflection among your class and may help them to retain information.

Materials required: None.

Notes: This works best with a small class, just because it can be time consuming to work your way around a larger class. It can be interesting to hear what students remember they've learnt! Use this to adapt your future sessions if what they've remembered from the session doesn't match your learning objectives.

How to use it: At the end of the session, ask each participant to state one thing they have learnt from the session (or how they intend to use what they now know).

Variations: For larger classes, try splitting them into groups and ask them to share one thing they have learnt with members of that group, rather than the full class.

Pitfalls: You sometimes get the same things repeated again and again as you go around the class. This may be because they are reluctant to volunteer information, or simply because they all took the same two or three things as most important from the session. If you've used it before and want to avoid this repetition you could try asking them to write down on a sticky note the 'one thing' they have learnt before reading them out.

Crossword puzzle

Uses: To check and review knowledge either at the start or end of a session.

Materials required: Simple crossword made up beforehand. Make enough copies for one crossword between two or three of the class. Answers should be key terms or names related to the training session. Create simple clues of the following types:

- A short definition ('A regular publication')
- A category in which the item fits ('A database available through metalib')
- An example ('Harvard style is an example of this')
- An opposite ('The opposite of plagiarised')
- Fill in the gap ('I can ____ books using the self-service machines').

Notes: Crosswords can be made larger or smaller depending on time constraints. Online crossword creators are available – such as *www. eclipsecrossword.com*.

How to use it:

- Split the class into groups of three.
- Distribute the puzzle to each group and ask them to complete it.
- Set a time limit and award a prize to the team that either completes it first, or has the most complete when the time is up.

Variations: Have the whole class do it together with a large version displayed on screen. An interactive whiteboard is ideal for this if there is one available.

Pitfalls: Don't get carried away thinking up cryptic or complicated crossword clues! If the clues aren't simple enough for most students to be able to answer them in the time allotted, then they are too hard.

Go to your post

Uses: To check knowledge and get people moving around, active and alert. Good at the start of a session or to wake people up further in.

Materials required: Pre-prepared signs – as large as possible, along with materials to attach them to the walls of the room you will be using.

Notes: Try to make sure you get a fair mix between the preferences or the discussion bit of this wouldn't work.

How to use it:

- Post signs around the room. They can be as few as two (so TRUE or FALSE can be used) or as many as you like that will fit in the room. These signs can indicate a range of preferences such as:
  - Topics of interest
  - Questions about content
  - Possible solutions to a problem
  - Personal values
  - Quotations relevant to the subject.
- Ask participants to go to the sign that most accurately reflects their preference.
- Each group of people at a sign forms a group – ask them to spend 5 minutes among themselves discussing why they chose that one and then give feedback to the whole class.

Variations: A really simple version of this can be used to check knowledge without discussion. For example, 'How confident are you at finding journal articles?' – Very much, a little bit, or not at all. This can then be asked again later in the session to check knowledge.

Pitfalls: Beware of health and safety issues. Make sure there is enough space in the room for people to move safely from where they are sitting to the prepared signs.

Hangman

Uses: To check and review knowledge at the end of the session, but including an element of competition.

Materials required: Flip charts or interactive whiteboard with 2 'hangman' type frames drawn on it (see diagram). A bell or a buzzer for each team.

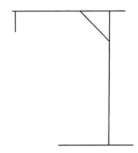

Notes: This works best with small groups so everyone gets a turn. It is important to have a brief discussion of each answer to re-enforce the learning.

How to use it:

- Split the class into two teams.
- Draw an example figure to show how many steps there will be (e.g. a head, body, two arms, two legs will give five points to lose the game. Add eyes, mouth, etc. to make it last longer).
- Get one member of each team to the front and give them a bell or buzzer each.
- Read out a question to them – the first person to ring their bell can answer.
- If the answer is wrong, that team gets a 'body part' drawn on their frame. If right, they can draw a body part on the opposite team's frame.
- After each question change the people at the front, making sure as many people as possible get a turn.
- The first team to get a full figure loses.

Variations: The player could call on another member of the team to answer, or pass onto the other team. Good at the start of a session as well as at the end, though it is easier to adapt at the end of a session depending on what time you have left.

Pitfalls: Try to make sure the groups are organised so they should be fairly evenly matched. If one side gets all the answers, the other team will end up demoralised. If it looks like one person is dominating right from the start, make them ask all the rest of the questions to even things up again.

I resolve to

Uses: To force members of the class to reflect on their learning and how they can apply it to their own situations. A useful way of reminding them what they have learnt at a set time after the class.

Materials required: A sheet of paper and envelope for each student.

Notes: This is quite a common way of encouraging people to think about how they can apply the class to their own situations.

How to use it:

- Ask the learners one at a time to tell you what they have personally learnt in the class.
- Write a list summarising what people have learnt.
- Give each of them a sheet of paper and an envelope and ask them to write themselves a short note saying what they feel they have personally learnt in the class and what they resolve to do or change as a result.
- Ask them to place the letter in the envelope and address it to themselves.
- Promise to send the letters on to them at an agreed point in the future.

Variations: Instead of individual letters, email or post out the summarised list at a set point (perhaps one month) in the future, with tips on how they can continue learning in this area.

Pitfalls: This creates extra work for you after the class has finished! Members of the class may resent being forced to reflect on their own learning, but it is an effective method.

I will do it

Uses: To force members of the class to reflect on their learning and how they can apply it to their own situations. To prompt them after the class to revisit their learning and remind them how they thought they could apply it.

Materials required: A blank form for each member of the class. The form should enable them to state the main things they have learnt in the class and what they intend to change as a result.

Example:

- What three things have you learnt in today's session?
  - (a)   ....
  - (b)   ....
  - (c)   ....
- How do you plan to apply this knowledge? Give a specific example and timescale.

  Timescale: ....

  Example: ....

  ....
- What will you do to continue learning about this subject? Give specific example and a timescale.

Notes: This activity, or variations upon it, is fairly commonly used. It can help turn the training or class they have just been attending from an abstract activity into something they realise they can and should use afterwards.

How to use it:

- Ask each member of the class to fill in the sheet listing what they have learnt and how they plan to use it.
- A month (or other agreed time period) later contact everyone who attended and prompt them to review their sheets. Have they achieved the task of applying the knowledge? Have they managed to continue learning about the topic? Include tips on finding out more on the subject area.

Variations: Collect in the forms and send them out after an agreed time period, together with tips on finding out more on the subject area.

Pitfalls: It means extra work for you after the class is over! While this is an effective method, often people attending your class don't like having to reflect on it immediately and put their thoughts in writing.

Lightening the learning climate

Uses: To create an informal learning climate by inviting the class to think about the subject matter in a creative way.

Materials required: None.

Notes: By making fun of a topic, or thinking of the 'worst way' to do things, the groups think about what is important as they go along – hopefully priming them for the formal teaching! Probably best with smaller classes unless you have lots of time for subgroups to give feedback.

How to use it:

- Explain to the class about an enjoyable activity you want to do before getting serious about the subject.
- Divide the class into subgroups.
- Give each subgroup an assignment to 'make fun of' an important topic or concept that you intend to cover in the session (e.g. '10 reasons why only Google is good enough for my assignments', 'Peer reviewed articles are no good for us because …', 'The worst way to look for resources for my dissertation' and 'Plagiarism: Why it makes my life soo easy').
- Invite the subgroups to report what they've done.

Variations: Present your own spoof of the subject matter at the start of the session – then get the class to feedback everything they spot wrong in the spoof.

Pitfalls: If they enjoy themselves too much, you may struggle to bring them back to more serious consideration of the topic. Make sure you build enough enjoyable activity into the rest of the session to keep them engaged.

Poster tours

Uses: When students have been working in groups and you want them to share their findings with each other.

Materials required: Flip-chart paper or similar one and a choice of coloured pens.

Notes: When groups are working on different aspects of a topic, this can be a relatively quick and painless way to share findings or thoughts out among the whole class. It is less intimidating than asking groups to come to the front and report to the whole class.

How to use it:

- When students are working in groups, make them put their thoughts/findings down on a large piece of paper (such as flip-chart paper).
- Each group puts their sheet of paper on the wall.
- Each group moves to the next group's poster and spends a short period of time (e.g. two minutes) looking at it/discussing it among themselves. They then write down their comments directly on the poster in a different coloured pen.
- The groups move around the room on your signal until each group is back at their own poster.
- The groups can then read those comments that the other groups have left for them.
- Give a few minutes at the end if anyone wants to share general comments with each other, or ask for any comment to be clarified.

Variations: An alternative but similar way of sharing is to use paper tablecloths – each group writes down their thoughts directly onto a paper tablecloth. These ideas are shared by moving tables.

Pitfalls: Try to make sure the groups have time to express themselves properly on the posters, preferably with you circulating and asking questions while they create them. If the posters express the thoughts of each group poorly, the activity will not be as successful as it sometimes can be.

Runaround

Uses: To check knowledge and get people moving around, active and alert. Good to wake people up in the middle of a session or to round off with something memorable.

Materials required: Pre-prepared signs as large as possible.

Notes: Try to make sure that the questions aren't too easy, or no-one will move when you shout 'runaround'! This is based on the 1970s children's TV programme – Runaround.

How to use it:

■ Post signs around the room. They can be as many as four or five as long as there is space in the room. These signs can either be letters (A, B, C, etc.) so they can be used several times, or listed specific answers (so can only be used once).

■ Ask participants a question (e.g. which source of information would be most appropriate in this situation: Newspaper, book, enyclopedia, etc.) and to answer it go to the appropriate sign.

■ When everyone has picked the answer they think is right, give them 30 seconds to 'runaround' between the answers. A short piece of dramatic countdown music can help to set the scene here!

■ Offer a small prize (such as passing around a bowl of sweets) to everyone at the correct answer.

Variations: You could use this at the start of a session just as well as at the end.

Pitfalls: Only try and use this if there is plenty of space for your class to move around. People falling over each other or furniture would turn a fun activity into a disaster, so check the room beforehand and only use this when you are sure it will be safe.

Stop, start, continue

Uses: A quick and easy way of getting feedback on your teaching.

Materials required: Sticky notes or A6 cards (preferably in three colours).

Notes: Standard feedback sheets often measure little more than how happy the members of your class feel and tend to be filled in either right at the end of the session or at a later date. This method is far more active, asking them up front to think about these three questions. It also asks specific questions about WHAT you are doing, rather than HOW they feel about it. As such it can often give good quality feedback on what you have included in the class, what they thought was good (so you can plan to do it again!) and what they thought was bad (so you can improve that element of the lesson before you run the class again).

How to use it:

- Give out sticky notes or cards at the start of a class.
- Tell students that you want them to think throughout the session what they feel you should:
  - STOP doing (so have done badly or inappropriately);
  - START doing (what you have missed out but they wanted); and
  - CONTINUE doing (what they thought was good).
- At the end of the session get them to hand back the sticky notes or cards with comments under stop, start or continue.
- If you have a large class, three different colours of card/note make them easier to sort through.

Variations: A traffic light theme would work just as well, with red for stop, amber for continue and green for start to match the STOP, START, CONTINUE above.

Pitfalls: As with any way of collecting feedback, it depends on the class being confident enough to share constructive feedback with you. Make sure they can fill in the cards and leave them for you in as anonymous a way as possible to help their confidence in giving you this feedback.

What about ...

Uses: Focus attention on the session at hand. Highlight common experiences, anxieties and expectations. Allows you to adjust your teaching according to the concerns of the class.

Materials required: Small piece of card for each student (A5 or A6).

Notes: If you expect to have too many students to sort through the cards quickly, set them another task at the start of the session (e.g. an exercise to check prior knowledge) to give you a chance to sort through them.

How to use it:

- Distribute a card to each student.
- Ask them to write down the main thing they'd like to learn from the session.
- Collect the responses together.
- Sort through the cards quickly and summarise them or read them out to the class.
- Answer any questions that you aren't going to cover in the rest of the session.
- At the end of the session run through the main questions and check that you have answered them to their satisfaction.

Variations: Use the learners' own mobile phones – ask them to text the main thing they'd like to learn to a number you provide for them. Again, you can scan through them to collate the questions and decide how to address them.

Pitfalls: If you don't manage to sort through the responses from the class and address them during the session, the members of the class with those concerns may feel more frustrated than if you hadn't asked what they'd like to learn in the first place. Make sure you build in enough flexibility to address everything that may come up, even if it is just to say you will provide more support or information afterwards.

What's your favourite?

Uses: A quick check of knowledge at the start of the session. To make the class realise as they enter that they will be expected to contribute actively to the lesson.

Materials required: A large piece of paper for each choice you wish to give the class (see below). A coloured sticky note for every member of the class.

Notes: This quick and easy exercise will help you judge the class as they come in and ensure you can adapt accordingly.

How to use it:

- Display at the front of the class a question you wish them to answer. You could use many different questions such as 'What is your favourite source of information? (Google, books, my friends, etc.)', 'How often do you use the library? (every day, once a week, once a month, etc.)' or 'What is your favourite database?'

- Put on the wall a piece of paper with a single choice on each piece in large, clear text.

- Ask the class as they come in to indicate which is their favourite out of the list of choices, giving them a coloured sticky note as they come past so that they can cast their vote.

- Summarise the votes when everyone is seated.

Variations: If you have an interactive whiteboard, you could ask them to tap their choice on the board as they come in, using the interactive functionality to count up the votes as they arrive.

Pitfalls: You may have to spend time explaining this activity as people come in, resulting in a slow moving queue and a little confusion at the start of the lesson.

In the middle

'In the middle' is our most general category, and our largest, covering tips that don't specifically fall into the other sections, but instead can be dropped anywhere into your teaching session. There is a real mix of different types of activities, including ways to encourage discussion, games to play and ways to bring music into your teaching. Some are quite specific, such as 'the model literature review', in the examples they give. The general idea behind them, however, should be readily adaptable to the range of topics you may find yourself teaching. The majority, however, we've tried to keep as generic as possible as it is hopefully easy to see how they are applicable to the sort of subjects we cover as teaching librarians.

You may find yourself using more than one of these tips within a class, as it's good practice to make sure that there is a change of pace or activity every ten minutes or so to maintain the concentration or focus of your learners.

Most of these tips are tried and tested standards of their type, albeit using library examples here, so you may already find that you use and regularly return to one or two of them. Even though these favourites may work for you, why not use this chapter as an opportunity to expand your options and try something different in your next set of teaching? It may just refresh your teaching once more!

Action cards

Uses: This technique can help to introduce an element of fun into the session. It will also help to keep the class active and alert.

Materials required: A piece of A5 or A6 card for each member of the class with an activity on it.

Notes: This is best done in a longer class that includes some group activities. The group activities provide a less disruptive time for doing the activities on the cards than when you may be talking to the whole class. It also means it is easier to add activities related to the session, e.g. 'show your neighbour what you have found in the Emerald database.' Activities don't necessarily need to be directly related to the topic, they will still help keep the class active and alert.
  Activities could include:

- Ask two questions in the session.
- Tell the person to your right the last book you borrowed from the library.
- Shake hands with the people either side of you.
- Change seats part way through the session.
- Help the person opposite with at least one question on the worksheet.
- Stand up and say hello to everyone in the room.

How to use it:

- Give everyone in the class a card with an activity on it.
- Tell everyone to complete their activity before the end of the session.
- Tell them that when they have done their activity they should pass their cards to the front of the class.
- You may need to remind people part way through the session to do their activities.
- Run through the cards at the end of the class (if you have time) and see if all of them have been spotted by members of the class.

Variations: If you think people might be reluctant to do the activities, get people to write their names on the cards before passing them back to the front and draw one at random to receive a token prize.

Pitfalls: This is a disruptive activity, so only use it if you are confident and have good enough classroom control skills to regain control if your class gets a bit too enthusiastic with some of their actions.

Anagrams

Uses: This technique can help to introduce an element of fun into the session. It will also help to keep the class active and alert.

Materials required: A sheet of library related (or related to the subject matter you'll be covering) anagrams for each person in the class.

Notes: This is best carried out in a longer session – in a short session they may well get too distracted trying to complete the list. If you think people are likely to get distracted in a session, this technique can provide an alternative focus that is at least related to the subject matter. There are plenty of free anagram makers online, particularly aimed at crossword enthusiasts. Just search online for 'anagram maker' or 'anagram solver.'

How to use it:

■ Give out a sheet of anagrams to everyone at the start of the session.

■ Explain that the anagrams are related to the subjects you are covering, as well as the general library.

■ Offer a small prize for the first person (or first two or three people) to complete them all, or the person with the most completed sheet by the end of the session.

■ Bring up a full list of answers onscreen at the end of the session.

Variations: If thinking of anagrams is too difficult, just scramble the words or phrases instead. You could include the anagrams down one margin of any handouts you distribute, to keep them visible without members of the class having to swap pieces of paper around.

Pitfalls: This can be a disruptive activity, though only at a fairly low level, so only use it if you are confident that you can deal with a few distractions.

Ask the expert

Uses: This technique can be used to enable the class to investigate several topics for themselves before explaining it to others in the class.

Materials required: A set of materials for each topic to guide each group towards the sort of knowledge you wish them to gain.

Notes: Make sure the materials you provide guide the students towards the knowledge they need (in other words, provide a 'scaffold' for them to work within), not simply provide a list of facts to learn. Knowledge gained through the students' own investigations will be richer than simply remembering facts that you feed them from the front of the class.

How to use it:

■ Split the class into small groups – as many as you have topics you wish to cover. For example, you may wish the class to learn about the different attributes of information sources (books, magazines, academic journals, etc.). You would need one group for each attribute you want them to investigate.

■ Give each group material on the topic you want them to become 'expert' on. This may be examples, worksheets, links to tutorials or any other information you wish them to consider.

■ Tell each group they have a set period of time (this will depend on the topics you are covering) to investigate their topic to become 'expert' in that area.

■ When the time is up, each expert group should take turns to come to the front for questioning by the whole class about their topic. You may need to help out for any difficult questions or to correct any mistakes made.

■ The class should make notes about each topic or area during this question and answer session.

Variations: Ask the expert groups to write up their findings on a blog or wiki so the whole class can share their knowledge at a later date. Instead of bringing the whole expert group to the front, get one member of each group to go to the next group along and share their expert knowledge. Give a set time period, then move them along, until each group has had the benefit of an expert from all the other groups. This is slightly riskier, as it is harder for you to tell where incorrect or incomplete knowledge is being past on.

Pitfalls: The two major pitfalls are if some of the expert groups fail to become 'expert' using the materials you give them or if the wider class fail to ask enough questions to extract this 'expert' knowledge. Make sure you are ready, therefore, to ask additional questions, or to fill in any gaps (and correct mistakes) when the 'experts' are being questioned.

Buzz groups

Uses: Encourages reflection and active learning, with the class expected to directly contribute their thoughts rather than the entire class having all the answers coming directly from the instructor.

Materials required: None.

Notes: This works just as well with large groups as small, even in large lecture theatres – just allow a decent length of time to share findings when you have a lot of small buzz groups in a large class.

How to use it:

- Split the class into small groups.
- Ask them to discuss a topic or answer a question.
- Allow a short length of time for discussion (five minutes?).
- Go round each group and ask a spokesperson for each group to share their discussions. This may be a summary of everything discussed, but will normally be to share one point to allow time to work around each group.

Variations: This can be scaled up – start with pairs, then groups of 4 (two pairs together), then 8 or 12, etc., to allow each group to share their discussions with a larger group. Try music to timescale the discussions, as suggested elsewhere in this book.

Pitfalls: For some groups it could be seen as an intimidating way for people to share the results of their discussions with the whole class, particularly with large numbers of people in a lecture theatre. In this case, 'scaling up' the groups can help, as you quickly get to a large enough group to be sure someone will be confident enough sharing with the rest of the class.

Class discussion

Uses: Useful when you really want some feedback and to try and gauge students' understanding. (When you think students are becoming too passive and reluctant to engage actively with the lesson and the learning activities.)

Materials required: None.

Notes: It can be really hard waiting for a response – don't worry if there is a period of silence before someone speaks up, just wait for them to break the silence first. A good reason for starting any session with some form of activity is to 'break the ice' and set an expectation that the class will be involved in their learning and feel safe to answer questions. This can be intimidating to some students who lack confidence to call out, even if they know the answers.

How to use it:

- Ask a question to the class.
- Tell them they can discuss the questions with their neighbours if they wish.
- Wait for answers.

Variations: Ask them to write their response down at the front of the class instead of 'shouting out'.

Pitfalls: This can be very hard to do, but useful when they really won't engage in voluntary discussion with you. You really do need to be brave and not break the silence first.

Countdown music

Uses: To timescale a particular activity.

Materials required: A piece of music of set length that is either copyright free or you are cleared to use for educational purposes.

Notes: This is a much more pleasant way of drawing an activity to a close than shouting to make yourself heard!

How to use it:

- Start your class carrying out any activity that you wish to last for a set time period.
- Let your piece of music start playing quietly in the background – not loud enough to disturb anyone, but loud enough to be clearly heard.
- When the music track finishes, make sure you don't let it go on to the next track!
- You'll normally find that when the music ceases, the groups will temporarily naturally stop talking and stop their activities, so you can then naturally draw the activity to a close.

Variations: For quick activities play music with a quicker tempo that naturally makes your groups feel there is a deadline approaching. If you're worried people may not notice the end of the music, try picking a track that slowly builds to a crescendo! Try playing music as people come into the class and then turning it off once you are ready to start. This will have the same effect and let you gently gain control over the class right from the beginning.

Pitfalls: Remember copyright rules! Don't use music unless you are certain that you aren't breaking the copyright law in your area.

Fill in the gaps

Uses: To let you provide lecture notes while still encouraging some active engagement in the learners' note taking.

Materials required: Handouts or lecture notes that cover the material you are about to deliver.

Notes: A small step towards active learning, rather than a large move. Even if the subject material is delivered as a lecture, the class will still end up more actively involved than if they have the full notes or a copy of the slides. On a personal note, when one of the authors was studying for their first degree it became the norm for lecturers to use PowerPoint and give out copies of the slides – even though the slides didn't contain enough information to revise from later, we all stopped taking notes! One of the lecturers quickly got fed up and started this method – his was one of the few the author had proper notes for.

How to use it:

- Prepare your handouts with certain keywords, phrases or small sections missing.
- Explain to the class you have put blank sections in, so they have to actively listen to the session and fill in the gaps.
- If you normally provide notes to people who have missed your lesson, make sure you provide the full version, not the edited one!

Variations: Instead of following the structure of your lecture, give out a sheet that lists the key topics you are covering with space in between for notes to provide structure and promote active listening for those key topics.

Pitfalls: This is still a small move towards active engagement with the material and you may find members of the class still 'switch off' and fill in the gaps later on by copying notes that others have made, if they bother at all!

Good search, bad search

Uses: Getting your learners to look at a 'real' search to try and identify elements that make it a 'bad search' and suggest ways of turning it into a 'good' search. This is a re-enforcement activity that would follow teaching on search techniques.

Materials required: A printed copy of a search about to be carried out in either an appropriate database or search engine. A second copy of the same search with the poor or bad elements highlighted.

Notes: Although the example here is for a search, this can be adapted for other activities such as referencing.

How to use it:

- After teaching techniques for effective searching, give each member of the class a copy of the example 'bad' search.
- Ask them to consider the example in pairs and highlight areas that could be improved.
- Run through each point at the front and discuss how the class feel the search could be improved.
- Give out the second copy with your notes on the poor elements highlighted afterwards for the learners to keep.

Variations: Run through the sample search live at the front and show the difference each change makes to the results.

Pitfalls: If you've chosen a particularly complicated search or specialised area, they may spot errors you hadn't meant to be there!

Library bingo

Uses: Any point where you may want to run through a list of items. Examples: inductions (what you might find on each floor of the library?) or sources of information (where could you look for information on ...?).

Materials required: A small piece of coloured card (A5 or A6) for each member of the class.

Notes: Brightly coloured card works well if handed out (or left on chairs) right at the beginning as it stands out and members of the class wonder what the cards are for! A small prize is nice for the winner(s).

How to use it:

- Give a small card to each member of the class. (This is probably best done at the start of the class before the session starts along with any other handouts.)
- At an appropriate time in the class point out these cards and tell them to write a small list (three to six) of things on it in response to a question. (For example – 'what different things might you find on fourth floor of the library?')
- Bring up a list of your answers to this question one at a time on screen. (Hint – do the *less* obvious ones first.)
- The first person to have all items on their list come up wins.
- Bring up the rest of the list.
- Ask if anyone has items on their list not on the screen and talk about the 'missing' items, whether right or wrong.

Variations: You can also play bingo by handing out cards at the beginning with words, phrases or pictures on (they all need to be slightly different to work). Give each student some stickers (small round ones) and tell them to put a sticker on each item as it crops up in the class. The first to complete their card wins. This technique ensures that they are paying *some* attention to you!

Pitfalls: If their lists are completely different to what you were expecting it can lead to quite long diversions from the material you intended to cover. Hopefully this won't be the case, but be prepared to improvise!

Making music

Uses: To get learners to represent what they know in a different, highly engaging way. Using the creative side of learners so they approach a topic in a different frame of mind.

Materials required: None.

Notes: Probably best with younger learners, or those more confident playing and performing! This can be quite time consuming, so may be best to consolidate learning between classes. They can then peform their resulting rap or chant at the start of the next session.

How to use it:

- Split the class into groups.
- Ask each group to investigate a subject area you wish to cover and represent what they've learnt by a rap or chant.
- Get the groups to perform for the whole class.

Variations: They could also create a music video using video cameras or their own mobile phones, especially if the task is set to run between classes. The resulting videos could go on your library web pages, VLE, or on YouTube – along the lines of this (*http://www.youtube.com/watch?v=NHiUQb5xg7A*) Dewey Decimal Rap!

Pitfalls: The resulting songs or videos may not be what you were expecting! If something offensive is created then shared among students or on the internet it may reflect badly on the library, so make sure they know what is and isn't acceptable beforehand.

Materials inspection

Uses: When you want to give students practice with real life examples rather than talk about the theory. When you want students to evaluate different sources of information.

Materials required: Originals or photocopies of a range of sources of information.

Notes: This normally works best if students have a list of characteristics to look for, so a template to work through can sometimes help. The final discussion can work really well if they have a topic or question that they need to look for materials on.

How to use it:

- Split class into small groups.
- Give each group an example of a type of source of information (e.g. peer reviewed journal article, trade journal, newspaper, encyclopaedia article, etc.).
- Ask students to look at the content of their item.
- Ask students to note down the characteristics of each item.
- Get each group to report back the characteristics.
- Discuss with them how each resource may be useful, bearing in mind the characteristics identified.

Variations: Make examples of different sources of information available for a topic and ask them to decide two of the sources that might be best for different uses (such as introducing a topic, getting ideas of current developments or a formal research topic). They can then list the characteristics of the items that make them believe they are most suitable.

Pitfalls: If the students haven't really thought about issues to do with quality or sources of information before, then they may really struggle with understanding what you want from them. This is where you may need to run through an example using a list of characteristics prepared beforehand.

Mind maps in action

Uses: Mind maps are a great way to help people come up with concepts and terms they can use in carrying out a literature review or just constructing a search strategy. This activity takes mind maps and makes it an active, group activity rather than an individual activity.

Materials required: Mind mapping software – either paid for or free (see notes).

Notes: Mind mapping was popularised by Tony Buzan (see his book *The mind map book* or his web pages at *www.buzanworld.com*), and is a way of exploring and expressing ideas by branching themes out from central concepts, dividing into sub-branches as often as needed and using colours, images and symbols where possible. There are many free and paid for software packages you can use to create your own mind maps. Some free resources available at the time of going to press are Bubbl.us (*http://bubbl. us*), MindMeister (*www.mindmeister.com*) and Wisemapping (*www. wisemapping.com*) though many more are available. Typically limited free versions of online mind mapping software are available that are good enough for most teaching, with extra features available for a fee.

How to use it:

- Explain to the whole class what mind maps are and how they work. One or two pre-prepared examples are great for this.
- Put up an essay title or research question at the front of the class in your chosen mind mapping package.
- Ask one person at a time to come up and contribute to the mind map. The first person should just circle the main concepts in the question, those following should contribute something extra to the map.
- Work around the class until people are running out of ideas.
- Show how they might take this map to help them construct a search strategy or structure a piece of work.
- Print out a copy of the mind map for everyone in the class (or make a link available).

Variations: If you prefer not to use a computer-based package, try using a roll of lining paper to draw a giant one on the wall. This could be shared afterwards by taking photographs of it using a digital camera and sharing these with the whole class.

The model literature review

Uses: Makes it easier for learners part way through a search of the literature to express and talk about the state of their literature review prior to a class on search skills, literature reviewing or finding different types of source materials. Encourages reflection on the current state of the learners' skills and knowledge.

Materials required: Enough building blocks such as lego® for each person to build a small model.

Notes: Works best with a small group. The model itself isn't particularly important. The model gives an opportunity for learners to reflect on an activity they've been carrying out and then talk about their model – rather than their activities in an abstract way. Make sure that there is plenty of time for discussion in the session, as well as time to dismantle the structure at the end of the session.

How to use it:

- Split the class into small groups, each of which has a bucket of building blocks on their table.

- Ask the learners to construct the current state of their literature search in building blocks.

- Give them five minutes to construct the model – they may need more time if they are wary of experimenting with the blocks.

- When the models are made, if time allows ask them to explain their models to the whole class. If the class is larger or there isn't enough time, ask them to explain it to the other members of their group.

- You are likely to find recurring again and again the same problems that large numbers of students tend to encounter. Make sure you listen to enough of the model explanations to focus on the key problems in the rest of the class.

Variations: This can be used in any situation where you want the learners to reflect on their existing knowledge or experiences, for example modelling their computer skills before an introductory class in a public library. Many different alternative modelling materials can be used, including children's modelling clay.

Pitfalls: This can be quite alien to some people and they may be scared of the activity. If so, try to ask for feedback from those people who are most confident in building their models first.

Please listen ...

Uses: To keep people awake and alert in the session! This promotes active listening in the class.

Materials required: A card for each member of the class with a word or phrase (related to the subject matter) printed on it. Each word or phrase should be on two of the cards.

Notes: It's best not to use a word or phrase you'll be using in the first few minutes! This can help make sure people pay attention to you in the hope of winning a small prize. Can be distracting if you are in 'full flow' when someone claims a prize!

How to use it:

- Give out a card to everyone at the start of the session with a word or phrase (related to the subject matter) printed on it.
- Tell them not to tell anyone else 'their' word and that there is at least one other person in the room with the same word.
- Tell them to listen out for anyone in the room saying 'their' word. If they hear it they should shout out 'My word!' as quickly as possible. The first person to shout wins a small prize.

Variations: You can either offer one small prize or carry on all session allowing people to win prizes. Carrying on until all the words/phrases are said works best to hold attention, but requires more chocolate/token prizes!

Pitfalls: This can be very distracting if you are delivering a full lecture-type lesson to a large class, but can liven up those short lectures you may feel you have to deliver between activities.

Quality or not

Uses: Great when you want to give students practice with real life examples instead of talking about the theory. When you want students to evaluate different sources of information and explore a range of resources.

Materials required: Some news stories, either from the TV, newspaper or internet news source reporting on a piece of recent research that has appeared at a conference or in a journal article. Enough for there to be a different one per group.

Notes: Can work really well with 'big' news stories on health issues. The category that often starts with 'scientist reports that …'. Make sure that the original journal articles can be found using at least one of the sources you recommend they use.

How to use it:

- Split class into small groups of two or three students.
- Give each group an example of a type of recent news story on research.
- Ask students to look at the news story and collect clues about the original research.
- Ask students to investigate the story using quality resources to find the real research behind the story – typically a conference report or journal article.
- Get each group to decide whether the news story accurately reflects the research or not.
- Ask each group to report back their findings and how they reached their decision.

Variations: For a more involved and longer term exercise, ask the groups to find their own news story from the past few months and investigate it using a set range of resources. This is riskier as the original research may not be readily available using the resources your library subscribes to. It also means the exercise is probably best run over at least three sessions so that they have time to select the story and investigate a wider range of resources to find the original article.

Pitfalls: They may not always be able to find the original research and could get frustrated – be ready to jump in with tips and advice if you really need to.

The recipe for a successful search

Uses: Getting your learners to reflect on their own experiences together with any other information you have imparted. To help encourage peer support and learning.

Materials required: A blank recipe card for each group.

Notes: Although the example here is for a search, the recipe card idea can obviously be easily adapted for any occasion where you want them to discuss how they may carry out a task.

How to use it:

- When discussing techniques for effective searching, split the class into groups and ask them to come up with their own group 'recipe' for an effective search.
- Ask them to pick a topic or give out pre-prepared topics – one for each group.
- The groups should list the 'ingredients' of an effective search first, then how they combine them into a recipe that gives good results.
- Each group can then feedback their recipe to the whole class.
- Allow plenty of time for discussion of the recipes afterwards, so the class give the main feedback to improve the recipes, with your guidance.

Variations: Create a menu instead – with starter, main course, dessert, coffee and mints etc. all being different stages of an effective search. If you want to introduce an element of competition, you could use a panel of 'food experts' to judge between the recipes (or menu cards), much like the UK TV programme *Masterchef*. Many different topics could be covered using the same techniques. Try using it for looking at the quality of different sources of information (one per group) or summarising a book in a reading group.

Pitfalls: You may need an example if they look blank after you set the task! Make sure you have one available just in case.

Referencing jigsaws

Uses: To help people visualise how to complete a reference and to encourage more active learning.

Materials required: Full references on card or laminated paper, cut down into their component parts.

Notes: It is easier if you use different coloured paper or card for each type of reference (they don't get mixed up as easily!).

How to use it:

- Split the class into small groups.
- Give each group at least one example of a reference (in its component parts) for a book, journal article, website or any other source of material you wish to cover. You could include 'extra' elements that aren't required as part of the final citation to make the exercise harder.
- Ask them to put together each reference in the correct order.
- Give a (small) prize for either the first team to finish or each team to get their answers completely correct.

Variations: Use an interactive whiteboard and get volunteers to drag parts of the citations into the correct order. Or give an item to a group of students together with cards for each element of the citation (e.g see below). Ask them to fill in the appropriate sections and then stand in the correct order for the reference as a group. Get their fellow students to say if they are right or not.

Pitfalls: If you've judged that their level of knowledge is completely wrong and they aren't able to do the task they can get quite frustrated. Make sure they are confident at having a go beforehand.

Show me, tell me

Uses: Enables learners to reflect on their current stage of knowledge in a way that accesses their creative side. Allows you to then adapt your session to suit the current group depending on the results of the exercise.

Materials required: Pots of modelling clay.

Notes: You don't need much clay per person. If the class is split into group tables, then one pot per table is likely to be enough. The important factor is making sure everyone has a pot within easy reach. The important factor is not the models, but forcing the learners to reflect on their current knowledge and to explain that to someone else. The models are just a tool to allow that reflection, so don't allow too long or the models will get more and more refined without necessarily any greater reflection.

How to use it:

- Distribute pots of modelling clay to the class.
- Give the class two or three minutes to model their current stage of knowledge (about the area you intend covering) or current stage of activity. This could be everything from the state of a literature review to what they know about searching the internet.
- Ask them to explain their models to the whole class.
- If any common themes emerge that you weren't expecting, adapt your session to take this into account.

Variations: Unless you have a lot of time, this works best with small classes. With larger classes, you could split them into groups and have them explain the models within the group rather than to the whole class. Various materials could be used for this – especially building blocks or bricks. Modelling clay is just cheap, quick, and easy to use and can quickly be cleared away afterwards. You could even ask people to draw using pencil and paper instead of creating three-dimensional models.

Pitfalls: This can be quite alien to some people and they may be scared of the activity. If so, try to ask for feedback from those people most confident in messing with the modelling clay first.

Spot the mistake

Uses: To bring some active engagement into those sections of a lesson that may be more didactic in style than you'd ideally like.

Materials required: None.

Notes: A small step towards active learning, rather than a large move. Even if the subject material is delivered as a lecture, the class will still end up more actively involved than otherwise. On a personal note, the first time one of the authors came across this method was in an A Level Chemistry lesson at school – the teacher used it in practically every lesson! It can be a novel challenge, especially for younger learners to try and 'get one over' you, the expert.

How to use it:

- During a section of your lesson where you are explaining something lecture style, tell your class you are feeling a little forgetful today and you may make some mistakes.
- Tell the class that they should watch out for mistakes and make notes of them.
- Deliberately introduce a few mistakes during your presentation.
- At the end, get the class to split into pairs and compare notes to decide on a list of mistakes.
- Work around the room, asking the pairs to contribute mistakes.
- They then need to correct any notes they've made to reflect the deliberate mistakes.

Variations: Give each student a piece of coloured card – the first to wave their card after each mistake wins a token prize of some sort.

Pitfalls: This is still a small move towards active engagement with the material and you may find members of the class still 'switch off' and either don't spot the mistakes, or more seriously, write down incorrect notes and don't correct them.

Washing line search strategy

Uses: Helps learners physically express the ideas of Boolean searching and different concepts or topics within a search strategy.

Materials required: A length of string and some small pegs for each group. A set of small blank cards for each group.

Notes: Small pegs can be found in many places these days, but if you struggle to find them, look out for ones sold as card holders near public holidays such as Christmas. Craft shops (online or on the 'high street') can be a great source of these sort of materials.

How to use it: After teaching about constructing a search strategy out of different concepts or topics from a research question:

- Split the class into small groups.
- Give a piece of string, some pegs and some blank cards to each group.
- Ask them to consider a research question and split the question into different topics or concepts.
- Tell them to write each topic onto a piece of card and think of other terms or keywords that might be used in a search. These should each be written on their own piece of card.
- Each group should then peg the keywords onto the line, grouping terms that describe the same concept together.
- Ask each group to explain to the class why they picked those keywords and what Boolean term would link those words pegged close together (OR) and those words in separate groups (AND).

Variations: A slightly more advanced version would be to put keywords within a group in order of how many results they would expect to find for each keyword, so introducing the idea of increasing or decreasing the number of search results by picking more general or more specific keywords. Sticky notes can also be folded over to stick to a length of string.

Pitfalls: It can be quite hard to explain what you want your class to do with an activity like this, so be prepared to leap in with examples if your groups start to go astray – don't leave them to it.

What animal are you?

Uses: Enables learners to reflect on how they currently behave and think about the strengths and weaknesses of that behaviour. This example addresses information seeking behaviour but can be adapted for many other behaviours.

Materials required: A copy per member of class of a list of animals that represent different information seeking behaviours.

Notes: Unlike many of the activities in this book, the authors remember where we saw this demonstrated! It was a conference presentation by two librarians (Borg and Stretton, 2009) from Sheffield Hallam University who have written about this activity and more in the article referenced below. We've listed the animals and characteristics they used, taken directly from their conference presentation and article, but these can obviously be adapted to suit your own classes.

Information seeking behaviour typologies:

- *Magpies* are easily distracted by the new and the eye catching, ignoring other relevant material.
- *Cuckoos* expect others to do all the work for them.
- *Vultures* are scavengers, not hunters, relying on scraps of information they find lying around.
- *Giant anteaters* use several sources of information, but do not spend long with each source.
- *Ostriches* avoid looking for information, especially if it might challenge what they already know.
- *Squirrels* rely on information which they have previously found and stored away.
- *Giant pandas* rely too much on a single source of information, even if other sources are available.
- *Orb weaver spiders* rely exclusively on the web!

How to use it:

- Split the class into pairs and ask them to discuss for two or three minutes a situation in which they had searched for information, in whatever context they wish – home, work or study.
- Give each member of the class a copy of the 'animal typologies'.
- Give the class two minutes to decide what animal their information seeking behaviour matches the closest.

- Discuss the strengths and weaknesses of each behaviour type, where possible starting by asking representatives of each typology what they believe them to be.

- This should then lead into advice and discussion on how existing behaviours can be modified to make the information seeking more successful.

Variations: This could be adapted for use wherever you wish to address current behaviours, for example in sessions addressing referencing and plagiarism.

Pitfalls: Trying to get people to discuss their existing behaviour may be difficult at times if some of the class are reluctant to admit to behaviours that may be seen as a weakness. If they do seem nervous and reluctant to discuss honestly their existing behaviours, it may be best to adapt the session so they do not have to share the animal typology they most closely represent with the rest of the class. The class discussion can then be asking members of the class to imagine they are a particular type and to think of the strengths and weaknesses that may imply.

Mobile phones and other gadgets

I wonder how many people reading this have signs dotted around their library either banning mobile phones or putting strict limits on where and how they can be used? However much we try to control their use, the typical library user (for most of us – prison libraries and libraries for very young children were the only exceptions we could think of!) is likely to own and regularly use a mobile phone. Across the UK, most of Europe, Australia and New Zealand there are more mobile phones than people, with the figures in North America rapidly catching up (International Telecommunications Union, 2009). In the developing world mobile phones are more readily available than fixed phone lines have ever been, leading to increasing expectation that they can be used to support and enhance an individual's learning and their interactions with libraries.

The mobile devices our library users have in their pockets or bags are increasingly sophisticated, not just able to make phone calls and send text messages, but to act as mobile computers and multimedia devices. They come equipped with cameras; can often be used to listen to podcasts (sound), watch vodcasts (video), run small programs (such as quizzes or QR code readers) and access the internet at faster speeds than may often be possible on their landline at home (through 3G networks or your library's wifi network). So why is our main reaction to ban them and hope they go away?

Learning using mobile technologies can 'create a powerful and engaging learning experience' (Facer et al., 2004: 400), the very nature of an active learning experience. People can be quite enthusiastic towards using their own phone in their learning, encouraging them to engage actively with the material.

There are problems associated with using users' own mobile phones related mainly to the different platforms available and the costs of making calls, sending text messages, and accessing the internet (Saville-Smith et al. (2006) have some nice practical examples of student comments on using their own devices). However, the largest barrier (costs) is becoming less of an issue each year as text messaging and even internet access is increasingly coming as part of contracted packages.

Other devices that your users may already have and carry with them (such as hand-held gaming devices, portable music and video players, and notebook computers) increasingly come with wireless internet connectivity, cameras and the ability to add programmes that mean they can also be used as hand-held learning devices. Your library may also have similar devices, whether they are general purpose devices such as mentioned above or more specialised teaching aids such as interactive voting pads.

These devices can bring an element of play into sessions and draw into active involvement in the session people who otherwise might have been reluctant to contribute. It always amazes us how much more excited people get when you pull out the interactive voting pads, even though the activity may be the same as if they were voting with coloured cards! International conferences such as the annual Handheld Learning (*http:// www.handheldlearning.co.uk/*) conference or the M-Libraries Conference (2009 conference website at *http://m-libraries2009.ubc.ca/*), as well as an increasing number of smaller, local conferences can be good sources of further ideas as the devices available and their functionality are constantly changing.

This section shows a few ways that we can take advantage of our users' mobile phones, other hand-held devices or more specialised teaching gadgets. None of them need disturb other library users or involve significant costs to the library or our users. Where mobile phones are used, it focuses on functionality that is available on the average mobile phone currently used in the developed world and is cheap or free for us to implement. As such, it doesn't really address the host of things we could do on mobile devices that require access to the internet, as this is currently (at the time of writing) available at decent speeds mainly on higher end devices with more expensive contracts, either through third generation networks (3G) or built in wifi cards.

The key technology we should be taking advantage of with our users' mobile phones is text messaging (SMS), which most of our users are likely to have access to at minimal costs and are comfortable using. As such, many of the following ideas use text messaging as their main medium.

Although some specific devices may be mentioned here and the bulk of ideas address the use of mobile phones, we would encourage anyone developing interactive teaching materials online to make sure they are easily accessible on the smaller screens of mobile phones, MP4 players and portable game consoles. You may find them becoming the main learning devices of the future – they already are in parts of the developing world where lack of fixed infrastructure means mobile devices are leapfrogging other educational technologies (Dutta and Mia, 2009)

References

Borg, M. and Stretton, E. (2009) 'My students and other animals. Or a vulture, an orb weaver spider, a giant panda and 900 undergraduate business students ...', *Journal of Information Literacy*, 3(1): 19–30.

Dutta, S. and Mia, I. (2009) *The Global Information Technology Report 2008–2009: Mobility in a Networked World*. Geneva: World Economic Forum.

Facer, K., Joiner, R. Stanton, D., Reid, J., Hull, R. and Kirk, D. (2004) 'Savannah: mobile gaming and learning?', *Journal of Computer Assisted Learning*, 20: 399–409.

International Telecommunications Union (2009) *Mobile Cellular Subscribers per 100 People*. 5 November 2009. Online at: *http://www.itu.int/ITU-D/icteye/Reporting/ShowReportFrame.aspx?ReportName=/WTI/CellularSubscribersPublic&RP_intYear=2007&RP_intLanguageID=1*.

Saville-Smith, C., Attewell, J. and Stead, G. (2006) *Mobile Learning in Practice: Piloting a Mobile Learning Teachers' Toolkit in Further Education Colleges*. London: Learning and Skills Network.

Instant podcasts

Uses: To allow members of the class to instantly share their thoughts and results of an activity with others, while capturing it to help later reflection. It can encourage the class to engage more with an activity as they have to express their thoughts in a way that makes sense to others. It can also make the act of feeding back results to the whole class more of a fun activity.

Materials required: A mobile phone per group. Increasingly people don't mind using their own mobile phones to support their learning, though if they do, you may have to provide one or more and pass them around the class.

A free account with AudioBoo (*http://audioboo.fm/*) or similar. In the fast moving world of these sorts of applications it is likely there will be many different similar applications to choose from by the time this book is published.

Notes: At the time of writing AudioBoo works best with an iPhone. An application is downloaded to the phone, recording of the podcasts takes place locally on the phone and the file is uploaded through the phone's integrated Internet capability. It is also possible to use it from other phones by ringing a number and the recording takes place at the other end of the phone line. If members of the class can use their own mobile phones to complete the activity, it can give a greater sense of ownership and achievement that handing around shared equipment for them to use.

How to use it:

- Set up an account with AudioBoo or similar.
- After students have been working together in groups, at the end of an activity, ask them to structure their results, thoughts or findings as a 60-second radio news report.
- Explain that news normally goes out live, so they will not have a chance to listen back to the report in their groups and then edit or improve it.
- Make sure they all are starting to record two minutes before the time is up.
- Provide them with details of where they can listen back to the podcasts afterwards. AudioBoo provides several ways of finding them, including downloading the podcasts from iTunes.

Variations: In the Web 2.0 section, we've included a similar activity using video cameras. Podcasts using mobile phones are quicker and easier, but increasingly video can be shot on hand-held learning devices like phones in a similar way to this activity.

Pitfalls: Groups can get drawn into trying to produce a funny or polished performance and end up running out of time. Make sure you stress the 'live' nature of news and hurry along groups that look like they aren't making progress well before they run out of time.

Mobile quizzes

Uses: It is always important to include knowledge checks as part of any lesson. Short quizzes via mobile phone mean your learners can also take them away and use them for revision or knowledge checking wherever they are in small chunks of time that suit them.

Materials required: A mobile phone friendly quiz creator! There are many available online, which tend to create quizzes in 'flash' format that can be viewed on most modern mobile phones. An easy to use one that will also host your quiz is Mobile Study (*http://www.mobilestudy.org/*) which is free to use.

Notes: Make sure you design the quiz carefully and test it well before use. Something that looks okay on a computer screen may not look quite as good on a small mobile screen. The size of the file created is also important – if the quiz takes too long to download, even those people not worried about data costs will be reluctant to access it. The example above (Mobile Study) allows you to download the quiz once (either via a computer or wirelessly), then use it as many times as you want, which is much preferable to one that requires constant access to the internet for the mobile device.

How to use it: Use any other way as you would to check knowledge during a class. Make sure you set up your mobile quiz well beforehand and test it works okay. It is best to get learners to complete a mobile quiz during the class if possible so that they are then more confident that they can access them again at a later date.

Variations: With many mobile phones it can be difficult to type in URLs to access the quiz. Try using a QR code (see 'QR codes for further information') to link directly to the quiz instead of publicising the full URL. Make the quiz available via bluetooth within your library to save on data charges for participants.

Pitfalls: Even though it is possible to download these mobile quizzes via a computer and transfer them to your mobile phone, most people are likely to go straight to the site via their phone. This means that people with slow, costly or non-existent internet access via their phone will not use the mobile quiz, though you may be able to help by using bluetooth networks to transfer the quiz to patrons' mobiles.

Online discussion by blog/phone

Uses: Allows and encourages discussion either within a physical class or at a distance. Encourages reflection on class activities and contribution by people too shy to speak out. Provides a platform for discussion results that can also work between classes or for distance learners.

Materials required: A mobile friendly blog that is set up just for the class with a service such as Moblog (*www.moblog.net*) or Jaiku (*www.jaiku. com*). A channel or group (terminology varies between services) for the class within the service. A class in which all have mobile phones and are willing to use text messaging to actively engage in their learning.

Notes: When working with distance learners, it is often hard to get discussion going. This method will work just as well for these learners as for those within the room. It will work for both synchronous and asynchronous discussions.

There are plenty of different choices for hosting a blog, services such as Moblog and Jaiku are those specifically designed to be mobile phone friendly. Services such as these allow mobile blogs to be set up and contributed to via SMS. Once registered, users can post to shared groups or channels. This allows text messages from many users to be pulled together in one place and easily viewed via a connection to the internet.

These microblogging services can be used as a way of reporting back discussions in class, or as an anonymous way of students answering questions, with the mobile blog group or channel displayed on a screen at the front of the class, much as dedicated audience response systems are used widely in education today.

They have, however, much more potential with distance learning students, allowing people to contribute to group discussions from any location, whenever they feel inspired to make a contribution. Contributors to these group discussions do not need to be in a particular spot at an exact time, they can take part effectively just as easily on a crowded bus or train on the way to work as if they were sitting at a desk or in a classroom.

How to use it:

- Set up a blog for the class with a service such as Moblog or Jaiku.
- Encourage members of the class to sign up to these services before the session with their own mobile phones and register for the appropriate channel or group.

- Encourage discussions, feedback from activities or general comments through the blog during the lesson, making the results visible online at the front of the class at appropriate points. This is done via text message (SMS), but could also be done through most internet capable device such as PC, laptop or gaming console.

Variations: You could also use an even briefer (and currently more popular) mobile blogging service, Twitter (*www.twitter.com*), which allows users to 'follow' each other, or use keywords in posts (prefixed by a # symbol) that can easily be pulled together in one place.

Pitfalls: They may be reluctant to sign up to such services beforehand, so you may have to allow time (and equipment) for people to register at the start of a class.

QR codes for further information

Uses: Instead of a static handout of lecture notes or further information, using QR codes can link the mobile phones of learners with a range of information they can interact with, including text, websites, videos and quizzes.

Materials required: Use whatever handouts you'd normally give out as part of your session but include a QR code. These are matrix codes, like a kind of 2D barcode.

Notes: You can find many free QR code generators online via your favourite web search engine. They all follow an international standard, so should be compatible with each other.

QR codes can be read by most camera phones, but need a free piece of software installed on them. A handful of mobile phones come with this ready installed, but most will need it installed by the user. If you go onto a search engine, put the model number of a phone in, plus the phrase 'QR reader', and it will normally bring back a link to a suitable piece of software if one is available for that model.

The codes either link to text or a URL, prompt the phone to send a text message or make a phone call. The ability to link to a URL is the most useful, meaning you can link to further information on the web, including videos and online quizzes that will work with mobile phones. This means that your learners interact with the extra information you are providing them with, instead of just having a static printed handout.

How to use it:

- Set up a QR code to link to further materials like (mobile friendly) video, quizzes or websites with more information.
- Print a QR code on your handouts.
- Include basic information on QR codes – enough for your learners to be able to find a free reader for their phone.

Variations: There are many different things you could do with QR codes – see Walsh (2009) for more ideas.

Pitfalls: Awareness of QR codes is low outside Japan, so first of all make sure most of your learners have camera phones, then provide basic information on your handouts on how to obtain a reader. The novelty will often prompt them to investigate the information you link to via QR code more than they would have investigated normal printed information.

To access internet-based information via a mobile (the mobile web), you need a mobile phone capable of accessing data at a decent speed – either a third generation (3G) device or one that can link to wifi networks. Data connections can sometimes cost extra over and above standard monthly agreements, so make sure you warn users of this possible cost. You should make sure that the extra information is available from a normal PC and provide the links so that no-one misses out.

Reference

Walsh, A. (2009) 'Quick response codes and libraries', *Library Hi Tech News*, 26 (5): 7–9.

Quick vote

Uses: To check knowledge and understanding with minimal effort.

Materials required: Interactive handsets (clickers).

Notes: This is an easy way to make use of interactive handsets throughout any session. Don't do it too many times however, or it may dominate the lesson. The interactive handsets make the responses anonymous, which can help overcome some people's reluctance to contribute. They are also fun to use, especially if used sparingly.

How to use it:

- At any point in the lesson where you would like to check that the class understands the topic, bring up a slide with a chance to vote on a question. This can be multiple choice or simply YES/NO or TRUE/FALSE.

Variations: For the same method without relying on any sort of complicated technology, use cards (coloured for ease of use) or simply a show of hands. These, however, don't have the advantage of allowing anonymous response.

Pitfalls: These sorts of interactive handsets (clickers) can sometimes be fiddly and time consuming to set up, requiring software to be installed and set up on the computer you are using as well as handsets being registered at the start of the class. If you use these in any lesson, make sure you have time before the lesson starts to ensure everything works, or you could have an embarrassing five minutes sorting out problems at the start of the session!

SMS discussion at a distance

Uses: If you're teaching a series of classes or delivering to distance learner students, it can be hard to maintain learning between sessions. Get them actively involved by encouraging discussion via mobile phone text message (SMS) either during class (especially for distance learners) or between classes.

Materials required: The easiest and cheapest method of enabling this method is via mobile friendly blogging sites. Key ones at present include Jaiku (URL), Moblog (URL) and Twitter. A free account for each learner with one of these services is all that is required.

Notes: Peer support and learning can really be helped through this method. It allows people to contribute to discussions anywhere they have their mobile phone with them: even if they have a few minutes on public transport they can send their thoughts to the rest of the group using these mobile blogging services.

The individual texts are pulled together on one webpage, so students still need access to the internet periodically (though that can be from web-enabled mobile phones), but can contribute between times without this access. It frees them up from having to contribute at set times or places, letting them make valuable contributions when and where it suits them.

How to use it:
For Moblog or Jaiku:

- Create an account with the service.

- Set up a channel (name service) or group (name service) for the class to use.

- Provide details of how to sign up to the service and the appropriate group or channel to your students well before you want them to use it – they may need support or encouragement to sign up.

- Set tasks between classes that need group discussion. Learners can post to the sites by sending a text message to a set number, starting the message with a keyword that directs the message to the appropriate channel or group.

- Everyone can then view the discussion from a website, even though access to this is not required to contribute.

- Regularly review the messages to make sure all of your class are contributing, as you would with any discussion.

For Twitter: As above, but instead of using set channels or groups, your class can either 'follow' each other (which can be complicated set up) or use a set keyword prefixed by the # symbol. It is fairly easy to then draw together all the messages in one place by searching for tweets with the appropriate keyword.

Variations: You can also set up 'conference call' style discussions, where users can call a number at a pre-agreed time and discuss a topic together without having to come into a fixed location. There are many different systems available, both commercial and free, that allow you to do this. Look out for ones that allow you to easily record the conversation – group members can then listen to the discussion afterwards to remind themselves what was said.

Pitfalls: The key pitfall is making sure everyone is set up with the appropriate service and channel/group. If you're worried about this, try to get them to register when you have them physically together in one place – this can save a lot of chasing around and support later on!

Text tips and reminders

Uses: Helpful for distance learners or to keep momentum up between a series of lectures. At the workplace of one of the authors, we used them to give a series of tips on using the library as an extension to the normal library induction.

Materials required: A text portal. These allow you to text messages to large numbers of students at once. You may find that your email server is capable of sending out text messages, particularly in large organisations, but these may only cope with small numbers of text messages at a time. Text portals may be available at specially agreed rates for educational use. For instance the JanetTxt service has arranged set prices for UK educational institutions.

Notes: Remember that text messages are brief – only 160 characters, so plan for short tips and reminders, don't aim to fit in depth material into a text message!

How to use it:

- Write a series of text messages and plan when they will go out. Make sure the tips you send out have a natural progression to them and match up with when they are likely to be required – for example we sent out tips on renewing books in the second or third week of term, the most likely time for books needing renewing the first time.

- Ask your learners to sign up to the service – making it clear how many they will receive and that they can opt out at any point.

- Most text portals will allow you to create 'groups' of users – put all your subscribers into one group.

- Send out texts according to your plan. Though you have flexibility, don't be tempted to send extra texts – your subscribers may feel they are getting too many and withdraw.

Variations: Use this system to send reminders out to groups of users before sessions, or links to extra material after sessions. For example, see Walsh, Andrew (2010) for ideas on supplementing a normal induction session with follow up text message tips and tricks.

Pitfalls: People can be reluctant to receive texts 'out of the blue', so don't set up this sort of service with information you may already hold on your learners. Ask them to 'opt-in' instead, agreeing to receive texts. Make sure you take care of your learners' mobile phone numbers. They should have the right to have their number removed from your list whenever they wish and it is good practice to delete the records once the series of texts have been delivered.

TV games – Who wants to be a millionaire?

Uses: Get more active learning into the session. Encourage competition between the members of the class.

Materials required: A set of interactive handsets (sometimes known as 'clickers').

Notes: Good to use at the middle or at the end of a session to see what has sunk in. Warn students early on that there will be a 'test' or quiz (preferably with prizes!). If you want it to look like the 'real' TV programme, there are freely available templates on the internet for PowerPoint (such as *www.primaryresources.co.uk/online/powerpoint/ millionaire_template.ppt*).

How to use it:

- Produce a set of multiple choice questions before the class ranging from really easy to very hard.
- Set the questions up in a set of PowerPoint slides to use with the handset's software. Set a 'value' on each question and have them run in sequence from £100 to £1m.
- Split the class into two halves.
- Get each half to send a volunteer to the front *before* you bring each question up.
- The volunteer should use their handset to answer the question. Alternatively they can nominate a friend to answer for them, ask the audience (their whole team), or choose 50/50 to have the possible answers halved.
- You can check which volunteer has answered correctly by setting up the handsets so they send a tick or cross to the handsets.
- The team that gets furthest wins a token prize.

Variations: Have two sets of questions and get one team to work through the questions first. Add one 'pass' option (or 'life') so a team can pass on one question in the quiz. Many TV game shows could be adapted like this – especially reality TV type shows. Again, a 'low tech' option can use coloured or labelled cards to answer the questions, if you think the class would appreciate the format.

Pitfalls: These sort of interactive handsets (clickers) can sometimes be fiddly and time consuming to set up, requiring software to be installed and set up on the computer you are using as well as handsets being registered at the start of the class. If you use these in any lesson, make sure you have time before the lesson starts to ensure everything works or you could have an embarrassing five minutes sorting out problems at the start of the session!

Wall of text

Uses: To allow feedback from the class, run polls and quizzes in class. Can use in similar way to interactive voting pads, but isn't limited by set numbers of expensive handsets.

Materials required: A system to collate texts and display them on a central web portal. Some systems are available commercially, but systems are also becoming available free to education in some areas (see *http://www.votapedia.com/* for an Australian system). For larger institutions you may be able to persuade a programmer to develop a basic system for you, which will cost only an annual or monthly charge for an SMS portal which will sit behind the system and connect to the mobile phone network. Alternatively, ask around if any colleagues from other institutions have such a system, they may be willing to share, especially if you share the monthly charges! At the University of Huddersfield we managed to find a system developed for a locally held conference, which was obtained for our use by agreeing to share the monthly charges.

Notes: Some systems require a keyword as the first word of a text message, make sure this keyword and the phone number are prominently displayed or on handouts before you ask a question.

How to use it:

■ When you would normally ask questions to the whole class.

■ Students text their (short!) response to the number given.

■ This is displayed at the front via a web portal.

Variations: Some systems allow polls/quizzes to be run, these can be a quick and easy way to check knowledge throughout the session.

Pitfalls: Make sure you check mobile phone signal strength before a session, preferably across more than one network. It can be embarrassing to find that a large proportion of students can't use the system because one or more networks have poor signal strength in the room. Make sure you know your learners before using mobiles! Mobile ownership is impressive, with more mobile phones than adults in the UK, Australia and New Zealand and nearly as many in the USA. This doesn't mean that everyone will be willing to use them to take part in teaching sessions. Some children and teenagers may see the expense of sending a text as a barrier, though most adults, particularly young adults, see the cost as insignificant, particularly if they have a set number of texts available as part of a package. Older adults may again be unwilling to interact with their mobile phones in this way, even though they are likely to own one.

Web 2.0

This is a slightly different section from the other practical example sections, in that there is a lot of overlap in the use to which many of these Web 2.0 technologies can be put. So, for instance, in reading a tip that suggests a way in which a video can be made and shared using a resource such as YouTube, please bear in mind you may be able to do something very similar using audio only and podcasting software.

Web 2.0 is typed by user generated content. These technologies allow people without technical skills to contribute something online quickly and easily and share these with others. They often also have a large element of social interaction built in, making it easy to share content with others, comment or rate content and connect to people with similar interests. This makes the Web 2.0 type tools attractive for sharing materials or discussions from a class and making them available afterwards.

Most of these tools are free for us to use and are often paid for by advertising, so if this is a concern you may wish to look at services that offer advertisement-free versions either for educational institutions or for a small charge. Web 2.0 services are also constantly changing, so though we give specific examples in the chapter, most of these show how to use the tools available in a fairly generic way, rather than focussing too much on unique functionality of individual services that may have disappeared by the time this book is published! Many people share their ideas for using Web 2.0 through the library literature, particularly through blogs, so it is worth using your favourite search engine to search for recent examples using current tools that you can adapt to your own use.

There are many different types of Web 2.0 tools, including photo sharing sites, video sharing sites, blogs, micro or mobile blogs, wikis, social networking, social bookmarking, custom start pages, podcasting and more, with some tools covering more than one type of functionality. As stated above, the services available change all the time, but a few major resources are given below.

The Web 2.0 tools and suggestions in this chapter can be a great way to generate resources that the class can continue to refer to (and possibly contribute to) after the formal teaching has finished. They can act as a way for the class members to revise what they've learnt afterwards, at the point at which they need to use that knowledge. It can also be a great way of generating enthusiasm for the subject past the end of the teaching session, with class members able to show colleagues, friends and family work such as videos or sets of pictures that they have created during the session, keeping the learning fresh in their minds. Lastly, many of the people you teach may be using these tools already in their personal lives. By bringing these often familiar tools into your teaching you can increase the perceived relevance of your classes to those students.

Some major Web 2.0 tools:

- *Photo sharing* – Flickr (*www.flickr.com*), Picassa (*http://picasa.google. com*), Photobucket (*http://photobucket.com/*).

- *Video sharing* – YouTube (*www.youtube.com*), Viddler (*www.viddler. com*), Vimeo (*www.vimeo.com*).

- *Blogs* – Blogger (*www.blogger.com*), LiveJournal (*www.livejournal. com*), WordPress (*http://wordpress.com/*).

- *Micro/mobile blogs* – Jaiku (*www.jaiku.com*), Moblog (*www.moblog. net*), Twitter (*http://twitter.com/*).

- *Wikis* – PBWiki (*http://pbworks.com/*), Wetpaint (*www.wetpaint. com*), Zoho Wiki (*http://wiki.zoho.com/*).

- *Social networking* – Beebo (*www.bebo.com*), Facebook (*www. facebook.com*), MySpace (*www.myspace.com*).

- *Social bookmarking* –Delicious (*http://delicious.com/*), Diigo (*http:// www.diigo.com*), StumbleUpon (*http://www.stumbleupon.com/*).

- *Start pages* – iGoogle (*http://www.google.com/ig*), Netvibes (*www. netvibes.com*), Pageflakes (*www.pageflakes.com*).

- *Podcasting* – Audacity (*http://audacity.sourceforge.net/*), AudioBoo (*www.audioboo.com*), Evoca (*www.evoca.com*).

... and now for the news

Uses: Sharing the results of an exercise with others and capturing it to help later reflection. Encourages the class to engage more with an activity as they have to express their thoughts in a way that makes sense to others. Making the (sometimes scary) activity of feeding back results to the whole class a fun activity.

Materials required: A video camera per group. This can be a dedicated camera, webcam attached to a laptop or any other video capable device. Quality isn't as important as ease of use – if phones with video capable cameras are widespread in your group, they could use their own phones to record the video.

Notes: At the time of writing this, YouTube (*www.youtube.com*) is the major worldwide video sharing site. It is increasingly mobile phone friendly and makes it fairly easy to upload videos from mobile devices such as camera phones as well as laptops and desktop computers which have an internet connection. It is free to view and upload videos on the site. With a YouTube account you have your own channel, so if all members of the class use the same account the videos will be easy to find as they will all sit under this channel. If you want them to set up their own accounts, then make sure you specify what tags they assign to them (to make them easy to find) and give you links to them so you can share these links to the videos easily amongst the class.

How to use it:

- Set up an account with a video sharing site such as YouTube.
- When students have been working together in groups, at the end of an activity ask them to structure their results, thoughts or findings as a 60 second news report.
- Give out one video camera per group and explain they have 10 minutes to write a news report, rehearse it and record it on camera.
- Explain that news normally goes out live, so they will not have a chance to watch the video in their groups and then edit or improve it.
- Make sure they are all starting to record two minutes before the time is up.
- Collect the video from each group. If they are using cameras attached to a computer, they can upload the result directly to a video sharing

site using the account you previously set up. Otherwise upload them yourself to the site.

■ Tell them how to find the videos and encourage them to watch and comment on them after the class has finished.

Variations: If time allows or lack of cameras dictates, use one video camera at the front of the class and ask the groups to come to the front one at a time and record their news programme with the whole class watching. This is more time consuming, but has the benefit of allowing discussion immediately.

If you are worried about content being publicly available, you may be able to put the videos on your own library's server for later viewing by the group. This makes it much harder, however, for the class to view them, reflect on the process, and leave comments.

Radio news can also work well, using free audio recording and hosting services such as AudioBoo (*www.audioboo.com*) that can work with any phone or free recording software that works on any computer (such as Audacity – *http://audacity.sourceforge.net/*) and uploading it yourself.

Pitfalls: Groups can get drawn into trying to produce a funny or polished performance and end up running out of time. Make sure you stress the 'live' nature of news and hurry along groups that look like they aren't making progress well before they run out of time.

Creating a pot of gold

Uses: Sharing resources found among the whole group. Giving the whole group a list of key resources they can follow up later. A way of discovering and evaluating resources for a project as a whole group.

Materials required: An account with a 'start pages' site such as iGoogle, NetVibes or Pageflakes. Quick guide on how to search for quality resources of each type you wish the group to use.

Notes: Instead of giving people a static list of useful resources or further reading, this acts as an interactive list of student generated resources, allowing the class to learn how to actively seek out and evaluate possible resources and share them with each other.

How to use it:

- Set up an account with a site such as NetVibes.

- Split class into small groups, except for one 'webmaster'.

- Explain that they will be searching for quality resources to help them with the topic they are working on and creating an online 'pot of gold' for them to use.

- Each group will search for one type of resource – this could include books (links to your library catalogue), general websites, blogs, journals, videos and more.

- Give them 15 minutes to find five resources of their type that they think will be of use. They should pass these on to the 'webmaster'. This person is responsible for putting a link (or embedding a video, etc.) onto the 'start page' you have created.

- Once their time is up, discuss as a class how they found searching for the different materials and the problems they had both in finding material and in checking it was good enough quality to be useful. This should give enough time for the 'webmaster' to finish putting the resources onto the page. With a small class you may not need a webmaster, and each group can put their resources directly onto the page. With a larger class you may have too many problems with multiple people trying to edit the page for this to be possible.

- Run through the resources as much as time allows – the ideal would be for the class to vote on whether they feel a resource is appropriate or not. In practice you may need to do this, perhaps even after the class has finished, deleting the inappropriate ones.

- Encourage them all to revisit the page in future to help them when they are looking for information on that topic.

- After the class, if possible, add some key resources they may have missed.

Variations: Use a social network, such as those you can set up yourself with NING to do something similar. This makes it easier for groups to contribute their resources directly, but makes it harder to view all the resources together.

Pitfalls: You may find that certain categories of information sources are easier to find material for than others – feel free to step in to help groups that are struggling.

Discussing results by blog

Uses: When students have been working in groups and you want them to share their findings with each other. Encouraging reflection on class activities. Providing a platform for discussing results that can work between classes or for distance learners.

Materials required: A blog that is set up just for the class.

Notes: When groups are working on different aspects of a topic this can be a relatively quick and painless way to share findings or thoughts out among the whole class that will work just as well if you have a virtual distance learning class as if you have a class physically in front of you.

There are plenty of different choices for hosting a blog, with many platforms freely available online, though sometimes you may have to put up with advertising being visible on a blog platform that offers free hosting.

How to use it:

■ Set up a blog for the class.

■ When the class carries out any activity in small groups, tell them to post their thoughts and opinions on the process straight to the class blog.

■ In any time you'd normally allow for discussion, tell them to read the posts of the other groups and leave at least one comment on another group's post.

■ Encourage them to read through the blog afterwards and post any more comments they want to at that stage. It then acts as a tool to reinforce learning.

Variations: In this form, the blog is acting in much the same way as asking groups to report their findings in front of the class verbally or physically written down (like in the poster tour). Blogs are a great way of adding in a way of them keeping the notes and aiding future reflection on their learning, so can be used in a similar way without the 'discussion' element of commenting on each other's posts.

Pitfalls: Try not to let them get obsessed with the technology aspect of blogging. They can add pictures if they want, but the look and feel of the blog entry is not important – the results of their activities and any reflection on them are.

Picture sharing

Uses: Sharing the results of an exercise with others and capturing it to help later reflection. Letting the class keep a visual record of their activity.

Materials required: A digital camera per group. This can be a dedicated camera, webcam attached to a laptop, or any other device with a digital camera. Quality isn't as important as ease of use – if camera phones are widespread in your group, they could use these.

Notes: The photo sharing site mentioned below is Flickr (*http://www. flickr.com/*) – there are others available, but Flickr is the major international player. It is free to set up an account and use it to host pictures. The ability to add comments to pictures enables the class to reflect on the activities after the session as well as the pictures acting as a visual reminder of the learning that has taken place.

How to use it:

■ Set up an account with a picture sharing site such as Flickr

■ When students are working together in groups, at the end of an activity ask them to take a photograph of the result.

■ Preferably ask them to upload the photographs themselves immediately to the picture sharing site. Otherwise, upload them yourself before the end of the class. If you want people to use their own accounts, make sure you specify a tag (keyword) before people start uploading pictures so that it is relatively easy to find them afterwards.

■ Tell them how to find the pictures, preferably showing them the site with the photos already uploaded, and encourage them to view and comment on them after the class has finished.

Variations: If you are worried about content being publicly available, you may be able to put the pictures on your own library server for later viewing by the group. This makes it much harder, however, for the class to view them, reflect on the process, and leave comments. Spend a few minutes taking the photographs yourself and uploading them directly. This has the advantage of added control, but the groups are less likely to feeling like they 'own' the pictures and have the interest in going back to comment on them later.

Pitfalls: The finished pictures may not reflect the end result of the activity very well, so it is important to encourage them to revisit the pictures and comment as soon as possible, while the activities are fresh in their minds.

Radio interviews

Uses: Sharing the results of an exercise with others and capturing it to help later reflection. Encourages the class to engage more with an activity as they have to express their thoughts in a way that makes sense to others. Making the (sometimes scary) activity of feeding back results to the whole class a fun activity.

Materials required: A way of recording per group – this may be a microphone and computer using free recording software (such as Audacity), or a phone linked to a free recording service such as AudioBoo. An account to host your podcasts – this depends on how you are making your recordings, but some podcasting and hosting options are given in the introduction to this section. Instructions for creating your podcasts.

Notes: This is a variation on the theme of making one person or group an 'expert' on a topic, then sharing that knowledge with the rest of the class. Podcasting the results as a radio interview is a fun way to share that knowledge (and to leave a record of that knowledge as a future resource for the class), but there are many ways to share this 'expert' knowledge – try some of the other options from tips given in this book!

How to use it:

- Set up an account with a service to host your podcasts and create a guide to creating podcasts and putting them on the chosen server. This depends on your equipment and personal preferences. Technology and services change fast to be too prescriptive in this tip!

- Split a topic that you want to cover in the session into a series of parts.

- Split your class into as many groups as you have sub-topics.

- Give them a set of material to investigate the topic themselves. This can be in any format you wish, from printed handouts, to lists of recommended websites, to interactive online tutorials. Make the learning objectives of each group as clear as possible.

- After a set time, the groups should each select an interviewer, who interviews the members of another group to explain the sub-topic they have been investigating. The interview should be recorded as a podcast.

- Show all the audio clips at the front of the class and ask for comments and further questions – the 'expert' group for each topic should try and answer any questions, though obviously you can help them!

- Tell them how to find the podcasts online and encourage them to listen to them and comment on them after the class has finished.

Variations: If time allows, or lack of equipment dictates, ask the groups to come to the front one at a time and record their interview with the whole class watching. This is more time consuming, but has the benefit of allowing discussion immediately. It also allows you to ask questions to fill in any gaps that are evident. If you are worried about content being publicly available, you may be able to put the audio files on your own library's server for later viewing by the group instead of creating 'real' podcasts. This makes it much harder, however, for the class to listen to them, reflect on the process and leave comments.

Pitfalls: Interviewees can sometime struggle, you may want to ask them to write their questions beforehand for you to quickly check so you can suggest more in depth or wider ranging questions to ask the 'experts'.

Sharing results by wiki

Uses: Sharing resources found among the whole group. Giving the whole group a list of key resources they can follow up later. Providing a scaffold for group activities during the session.

Materials required: A wiki set up beforehand that is open for others to join.

Notes: There are plenty of free wikis available at the moment, both to host on your own server and that offer to host them for you. They are often funded by advertising revenue, so you may find adverts displayed on the side of a free wiki unless you find space to host it yourself.

How to use it:

- Set up a wiki and structure it in a way that every group will have a section in the wiki to use.
- Each section of the wiki should have instructions for the groups to follow and provide enough structure for the groups to easily follow. The instructions should be directly related to the learning objectives of the lesson. For instance if you are teaching a lesson on assessing the quality of information found, then each section may include information on how to assess quality; instructions for the group to run a particular search and assess the quality of the top three results; links to further resources; and a section for them to edit and enter the results of their exercise.
- Split the class into groups and allocate each a section of the wiki.
- Spend time with each group as they carry out the activity, making sure they start to put their results into the wiki in plenty of time.
- Give time at the end for the groups to quickly look through the other groups' entries and give feedback on the activity.
- Encourage them to look back after the class and reflect on their own activity in light of the entries by the other groups.

Variations: Many of these Web 2.0 tools allow similar activities, giving a platform for sharing of discussions and activities that your class can then look back on and aid their own reflective learning. This activity works well as an individual activity for the class to do before your formal session, with remote advice via email (if you can persuade them to take part in it). The start of your formal session can then be discussing the contributions to the wiki.

Pitfalls: You need a good structure in place to guide people and make it as clear as possible what is expected; if not it will either fail or take up lots of time in class explaining it. Can get quite 'needy' groups, so can be quite time consuming to both set up and support people on it, especially if you want people to complete it in their own time rather than in a formal lesson. Once you have a basic structure that works, however, it can be adapted and reused time and time again.

That's delicious

Uses: Sharing resources found among the whole group. Giving the whole group a list of key resources they can follow up later.

Materials required: An account with a social bookmarking site such as Delicious (*http://delicious.com/*).

Notes: Instead of giving people a static list of useful resources or further reading, this acts as an interactive list of resources, allowing the class to actively engage and respond to your suggestions as well as contribute their own.

How to use it:

- Set up an account with a social bookmarking site such as Delicious.
- Populate it with a few key resources or links to guide the class to further help.
- Show the whole class how to log on to the resource and add links to it.
- In any activity that involves searching the internet for useful resources, ask each member of the class to bookmark (using the account you've set up) the three most useful they found, along with comments as to why they found it useful.
- At the end of the activity, talk through some of the resources and encourage discussion as to some of the best and worst resources found.
- Encourage them to revisit the site afterwards as a resource for their future work.

Variations: Ask groups within the class to investigate set categories and split the finished set of resources up by these categories, using either tags (keywords) you give beforehand or a separate page per category.

Pitfalls: You may find either a small set of resources repeatedly found by different people or inappropriate resources dominating the results. If so, it may be necessary to provide guidance part way through the activity to encourage a change in direction.

Twittering away all class long

Uses: To provide instant feedback to you as the class instructor. To let people ask questions anonymously throughout the session. It lets members of the class actively engage with you and the subject material even in periods where you may be using a didactic style of lecture between activities. Can be used where students have access to either a computer or hand-held device (including phones and gaming devices) capable of connecting to the internet.

Materials required: A twitter account for each member of the class. A laptop, phone or other device visible to you at the front of the class that you can keep twitter visible on during the whole session.

Notes: At the time of writing, Twitter (*http://twitter.com/*) is the undisputed leader of the 'microblogging' pack. It allows people to 'tweet' short messages of up to 140 characters that (normally) anyone can view. It has a strong social network side, with members 'following' or being 'followed' by other members, so you can form social networks where your followers are constantly being kept up to date with your activities via your tweets.

Its strength for this activity is its powerful live search. It can quickly and effectively search all live messages within Twitter and display the results in real time. This is often used at conferences where #tags are agreed that signify a message is about that particular conference and attendees include that #tag as part of their message. A recent example (at the time of writing) was the LILAC conference where the tag was #LILAC2010. Using the powerful live search facility people could search for #LILAC2010 to see messages about the conference as it happened, allowing ad hoc networks to develop. It is this sort of facility to develop an ad hoc network using #tags and Twitter search that we take advantage of here.

How to use it:

■ Provide information before the class starts on how to set up a Twitter account.

■ At the start of the class, ask how many of them have set up a Twitter account. If you *don't* have a high proportion, ask those without an account to set one up (using notes you should provide) before your lesson properly starts. This should only take a couple of minutes.

■ Put a #tag for the day's class somewhere prominently visible to the whole class.

- Explain that if they send a tweet contain that #tag during the class you will see it at the front of the class. If they want to ask a question, or need anything clarifying during the session, they can use Twitter to send it to you anonymously and you will try and address it before the end of the session.

- Make sure that you keep an eye on Twitter all the way through the session and address any questions or comments at appropriate points.

Variations: A text wall, where people can text (SMS) to a number and have it appear on a webpage, can also be used in the same way.

Pitfalls: If you have a bad relationship with the class it could degrade into a way of sending you distractive questions or abusive messages to put you off from teaching as they can effectively be anonymous and the disruptive member of your class does not have to worry about any comeback. If abusive messages come through they are easily ignored, but questions aimed to distract you from your point may be less easily dealt with. Remember to use your common sense, as you would with normal questions, and don't feel you have to answer everything if you don't feel it is appropriate to do so. You can always say at the end you haven't answered everything, but offer to go into more depth with anyone that needs help.

Inductions

Library inductions, or orientations, are something we often worry about, particular in Further and Higher Education libraries, where typically we can expect to see large numbers of new students coming through our doors for a short induction at the start of the academic year. This section is therefore included as a set of examples in this chapter, to show examples of more active inductions we can use. It is not strictly the same as the previous tips, which can normally be used for lessons on any topic, but follows the same format as those tips, as opposed to the full lesson plans that follow in the next chapter.

We all want to create a good impression of our own library, whether large or small, for our new users. We want to make sure these new users don't just get the basic information about the library, but also have any anxieties about coming into the library addressed, so that even the most reluctant users of our services feel comfortable returning to the library in the future.

With larger libraries, this is a particular concern, with new users finding the library an intimidating and confusing place. For certain groups of potential users, such as those with dyslexia, entering any library can seem like they are coming into a scary, alien environment and it can take a great deal of courage just to come through the door. As Collinson and Williams (2006) say, you cannot '...effectively train people and give them new skills until you have overcome the barrier of fear that many face...'. In their case they tried to alleviate some of this anxiety by providing a mixture of induction materials and methods that were as interactive as possible. Others have linked poor inductions with student retention (Edward, 2003) and used active learning techniques to try and give new students a better start to their university courses, successfully helping new students to be more comfortable in these new, potentially quite scary surroundings.

Possibly the ideal for a library induction is therefore an informal tour and chat with a knowledgeable and helpful librarian, preferably one-to-one, though at most with a small group of new users. This chapter is for those of us who work in libraries, probably primarily in education (schools, colleges and universities) where we have to deal with such large numbers of new users in a limited period of time that we could never hope to offer such small, personalised inductions. The desire to improve learning outcomes is of importance, but often the impetus to trying new ways of library inductions is lack of staff time to carry out such tours. The case study by Carpmael et al. (1992) is a classic example of this, showing changes in their inductions as staff struggle to cope with a 29.5 per cent increase in student numbers.

Even so, the tour remains a perennial favourite even in libraries with large populations. However, the tour has significant problems when scaled up to deal with large numbers of students. The groups tend to be larger than we'd like, so people at the back can either struggle to hear and see what is happening, or they can drift into chatting among themselves. The tours tend to be run at times when the library is busiest with new and returning students, so you can find yourselves competing with the crowds. It is also hard to keep up your own enthusiastic delivery by the time you've done more than a few tours, and the last groups you show around on the Friday of induction week are likely to have a different experience to the very first! Last, and not least, running library tours is incredibly time consuming and unlikely to be practical for all new users in larger institutions unless you are very generously staffed. Pulling in extra temporary staff such as student helpers can help tours continue, but this brings its own problems – we regularly despair at the errors we overhear that have crept into these tours! Often we fall into providing lectures to large numbers of students as they are more efficient in terms of staff time, even though they are less interactive and may provide a worse experience for the user.

A self-directed tour is a useful alternative to a guided tour or having a library guide (for instance Granger, 2003). This also brings elements of active learning into inductions while saving staff time. Other active alternatives reported in the literature include treasure hunts (Thompson, Kardos and Knapp, 2008) and a variation on the 'planted question' method of teaching, the Cephalonian Method (Morgan and Davies, 2004).

To induct more students without undue demands on their time and ours, the authors, in common with librarians in a range of workplaces, have looked at various alternatives over the years in our own workplaces. These have ranged between the extremes of large, impersonal mass inductions often run in rooms outside the library (such as lecture theatres full of students watching slide shows or videos) to individual workbooks or quizzes adapted for each subject area. The balance between staffing constraints and providing a rich learning experience for our new users (that hopefully breaks down any anxieties they may have about the library) is incredibly hard to achieve.

This section outlines a few alternatives to the tour, or standard talks to lecture theatres of students, that try to balance those conflicting demands. Hopefully one or more of them will help your new users get actively involved in their library inductions without exhausting you and your colleagues.

References

Carpmael, C., Morgan, S. and Nichols, J. (1992) 'Library orientation: a workable alternative?', *Library Review*, 41 (4): 16–30.

Collinson, T. and Williams, A. (2006) 'Library e-induction: alleviating anxiety with digital doughnuts: as case study', *ELIT*, 5 (4). 18 August 2009. Online at: *http://www.ics.heacademy.ac.uk/italics/vol5iss4/collinson-williams.pdf*.

Edward, N. (2003) 'First impressions last: an innovative approach to induction', *Active Learning in Higher Education*, 4 (3): 226–42.

Granger, J. (2003) *DIY Induction: Developing an Active Learning Programme in the Harrison Learning Centre*. CELT Learning and Teaching Projects 2002/03. 18 August 2009. Online at: *http://hdl.handle.net/2436/5261*.

Morgan, N. and Davies, L. (2004) 'Innovative library induction: introducing the "Cephalonian method" ', *SCONUL Focus*, 32 (Summer/Autumn): 4–8.

Thompson, K., Kardos, R. and Knapp, L. (2008) 'From tourist to treasure hunter: a self-guided orientation programme for first-year students', *Health Information and Libraries Journal*, 25: 69–73.

Walsh, Andrew (2010) Supplementing inductions with text messages, an SMS 'tips and tricks' service. *ALISS Quarterly*, 5(3). pp. 23–25. Online at: *http://eprints.hud.ac.uk/7393/*.

Cephalonian induction

Uses: As a way of introducing an element of humour into inductions, as well as an easy introduction to a class taking an active part in their own learning. To break up the structure of a standard induction and make it fresh again for the instructor.

Materials required: Set of slides and projector. A question card covering each slide, preferably laminated for re-use. A list of questions cross-referenced with the number of the slide they refer to.

Notes: This method, that uses the idea of planting questions in the audience, has rapidly become popular since Nigel Morgan and Linda Davies first described how they developed it for use with medical and biological students at Cardiff University (Morgan and Davies, 2004).

It uses music (as people enter and leave the session), humour, audience participation and an element of flexibility in delivery to keep inductions 'fresh' for the person delivering inductions as well as appealing to the students.

How to use it:

- Prepare a slide for each topic you'd normally cover in your induction.

- For each slide prepare a question on a laminated sheet of paper that links up with the details on that slide. For example, 'It's raining and I can't possibly get my hair wet. Can I access information to complete my assignments from home?' may link to a slide on accessing library resources from home. Try to make the questions light hearted or humorous.

- On a sheet of paper list the questions and the number of the slide that links with that question.

- Play music (within copyright rules, of course!) as people enter and leave the session.

- When your class enters the room for their induction, give out any handouts, but include the questions spread out among the class.

- Tell them that certain 'lucky people' have a question card within their handouts.

- Invite one question at a time from the class.

- For each question, check on your list what number slide matches up and jump to that slide on screen (in Microsoft Powerpoint, just type the slide number then press <ENTER>).

- Cross each question off your list as it is asked. At the end check your list to make sure no questions are left (from anyone too shy to read one out or pass it to their neighbour!). If there are any left, cover this material at this stage.

Variations: The original method split their questions into four categories (basic introductory information, finding items on reading lists, services and facilities and miscellaneous) and assigned each of them a colour. They then asked for questions within one particular colour at a time (e.g. 'Could we have a yellow question please?') which helped impose structure on the session.

Pitfalls: If it is obvious you are handing out the questions at the start you may find people refusing to accept them. I find it often works best hiding them in a pack of other information – students can then swap among themselves if they don't want to answer a question.

Some classes can be reluctant to ask questions at all. If so, don't struggle asking for volunteers – you still have the slides to revert to a more traditional lecture style of induction!

To make this a success you must be confident and flexible in the way you deliver your teaching. If you need more structure to your classes, or struggle to ad lib in response to sometimes unexpectedly adapted questions, then this method is probably not suitable for you.

Induction by crossword

Uses: To encourage an enquiry-based learning approach to library inductions. To bring an element of fun to an often dry, boring activity.

Materials required: A simple crossword made up beforehand. Make enough copies for one between two or three of the class. Answers should be key terms or names related to using the library. Create simple clues of the following types:

- A short definition ('A way of finding what books the library holds').
- A category in which the item fits ('A database available through our webpages').
- An example ('Harvard style is an example of this').
- An opposite ('The opposite of plagiarised').
- Fill in the gap ('I can ____ books using the self-service machines').

Notes: Crosswords can be made larger or smaller depending on time constraints. Online crossword creators are available – such as *www. eclipsecrossword.com*. Make sure you include a question for everything you'd normally cover in a library induction.

How to use it:

- Cover any material *not* included in the crossword at the start of the session.
- Split the class into groups of three.
- Distribute the puzzle to each group and ask them to complete it.
- Set a time limit and award a prize to the team that either completes it first or has the most complete when the time is up.
- Make sure everyone has access to the answers at the end and run through some of the most important answers.

Variations: Have the whole class do it together with a large version displayed on screen. An interactive whiteboard is ideal for this if there is one available. Any activity that involves the learners searching out information for themselves, so short worksheets would also work; as would 'open' quizzes where teams have a time limit to find an answer and vote using interactive voting pads or mobile phones.

Pitfalls: Don't get carried away thinking up cryptic or complicated crossword clues! If the clues aren't simple enough for most students to be able to answer them in the time allotted, then they are too hard.

Induction competition

Uses: To encourage an enquiry-based learning approach to library inductions. To bring an element of fun to an often dry, boring activity. To bring some physical activity into library inductions.

Materials required: Set of questions, at least one for each area you would normally cover in a library induction. These should be put on A5 or A6 cards, one question per card, and laminated. You need enough sets of these questions for one between two or three of your largest expected class. The same number of dry wipe pens as you have sets of questions. Enough handbooks, library guides or computers accessing your library website to allow everyone in the class to investigate the answers themselves.

Notes: This takes a while to produce the cards, but they can then be re-used time and time again, so worth an initial effort. This type of activity tries to encourage learners to actively engage with the existing material the library produces, so even if they forget much of what they learn in the induction, hopefully they will remember where to find the answers to all their future questions about using the library!

How to use it:

- Split the class into groups of two or three people.
- Give each group question 1 only.
- Tell them to use the resource you provide to find the correct answer.
- As each group finds an answer, they should write it on the card and bring it to the front of the class. If the answer is correct, they can swap the card for question 2. If wrong, they must take it away and try again.
- Each team to complete the full set of questions before the time limit should win a token prize of some sort.
- Five minutes before the time is up, stop the activity and pass around a full set of questions and answers.
- Ask if any questions seemed particularly difficult and expand on how those answers were and how you find them.

Variations: Do a similar quiz online, or as a mobile phone friendly quiz, where a question must be answered correctly to advance to the next question. If you can include in this a timed element with a 'high score' table of the fastest people to complete the quiz, it will keep this competitive element. The danger with using multiple choice type questions online or on mobile quizzes is that people will guess answers to try and speed through the questions quickly.

Pitfalls: This can be quite staff intensive for large classes, as you need to make sure large queues don't form of people waiting to swap questions over. If you can't provide enough staffing for large numbers in a class, use it for smaller classes or use online or mobile versions instead. Make sure you have plenty of spare pens as they will start to go astray or dry up fairly quickly if you use this method often.

Treasure hunt induction

Uses: To get learners out and about exploring the library rather than receiving lecture style inductions.

Materials required: A set of questions following a treasure hunt around the library. Markers at set points around the library containing a unique word or picture for the learners to prove they've found the correct answer.

Notes: Once you have set up the treasure hunt initially, it should only take a few minutes to check everything is okay before each induction. It is then a fairly quick and easy induction to run, particularly if you arrange for someone else to give them the question sheets beforehand and then reveal the answers online afterwards. You may only need to spend a few minutes at the end of the allotted time checking that no-one had any serious problems finding the answers.

This is also ideal for giving out for others to run, so once set up can be offered to others who may not normally send their groups to a library induction, thus involving more potential users with no more of your time required!

How to use it:

- List all the areas you would normally try and cover in a library induction.
- Put signs or stickers in appropriate places in the library that cover the areas you wish to include.
- Produce a set of questions that give clues to find the stickers or signs and have space for the learners to mark what they find. For instance if you wish to cover the fact that copying can be done on the ground floor for 4p a sheet, a clue could be 'This costs 4p a time on the ground floor'. A sign would be discreetly put near the photocopiers so they have to explore and find them.
- Bring your class together at a set time to run through the answers, or reveal them online a set time afterwards (i.e. so they can't look at the answers instead of exploring themselves!).

Variations: A mobile phone version could be done using Quick Response (QR) codes, with stickers showing different QR codes containing one of the words which together make up a sentence describing where to claim a small prize (perhaps credit for printing or photocopiers if applicable in your library). When they have found all the QR codes they can untangle the words into a sentence to find out where to claim the prize. This would of course need an alternative method if QR codes are not widespread in your institution. For a short explanation of QR codes, see the 'QR codes for further information' tip.

Pitfalls: Large numbers of students carrying out such a treasure hunt can be disruptive, so try not to have large numbers at busy times!

Virtual induction

Uses: When you have no time or space to see all the students you need to, but still want them to receive more active teaching materials than a leaflet or handout. Probably the best way to 'mop up' students you haven't been able to see face to face.

Materials required: More involved than most of these tips, this needs some serious website design!

Notes: This is not just the standard library webpages! There are many examples of these about – *www.hud.ac.uk/cls/thebasics* is just one recent example that combines all the elements below. Free software is available to create all the interactive materials mentioned here, often even as mobile versions for installation on a USB memory stick for those of us who struggle with IT departments when we want to get software installed on our work computers.

How to use it: To make this work you need to outline the material you would normally aim to cover in your library inductions and split it into topics or categories. Each of these categories should contain a mixture of resources to cover the material you've already outlined.

To make it truly involving and active learning, you should include a range of different resources to address different learning styles. It is fairly easy these days to create podcasts, vodcasts and interactive tutorials to support basic text and images on a webpage. As a minimum, however, make sure there are plenty of chances to check knowledge (such as brief quizzes) within or at the end of each section and include various ways for users to get in touch with the library to ask further questions.

Make sure that these categories don't follow a linear narrative – few people will have the patience to work slowly through a set of materials on using the library that will take an hour or more of their time. The best examples allow users to dip in and out of the material as they wish, both initially as an induction, and at a later date to refresh their knowledge.

Variations: This can vary as much as you like, but an easier, quicker version would be to use information from existing webpages and draw them together as an online quiz. The online quiz can link to the other existing webpages for them to draw together the required information.

Pitfalls: Can take a lot of time and effort to set up, but remember that this can be spread across a lot of students! You can't tell how many people from a particular cohort have accessed the site or not unless you add an extra barrier of logging in. This method is unlikely to reach as high a proportion of any group of students as most induction methods, as unless they are scheduled to look at the induction website at a particular time and place, only the keenest are likely to spend much time on the site!

3

Lesson plans

It is easy to slip into the idea that lesson plans are a waste of time, especially if we tend to teach only a small number of topics. You may think that you've done a certain topic several times already, so you 'know what you're doing' already and don't need to write a lesson plan.

It may surprise you how much things can change when you put time aside to write a lesson plan to address a lesson in even these familiar topics. They force us to think about what we'd like to achieve in a session and help us to express that to the class. They may help us to adapt a session to the needs of a particular group, so we don't simply repeat the same lesson ad nauseam to different groups with different needs. They can force us to think about assessment, that is, about how we know if the class have actually learnt anything from the session. If nothing else, they can make it easy to ensure we have all the handouts and equipment we need before we start!

The style and layout of lesson plans varies immensely, so you should use one that best suits your own needs. The examples given in this chapter are extended versions and would normally be summarised to fit onto one or two sides of paper, though we do give some examples of blank layouts to show the ways the elements below can be incorporated into a lesson plan template. You're likely to find that the information on your plans get briefer the more experienced you are in teaching a topic, as you can summarise more easily what you intend to do within a lesson. Ideally, however, make sure they have enough detail for someone else to pick up and use, so that if for some reason you can't take a class, someone else can use your planning. This will also make it easier to share lesson ideas and plans with your colleagues, so you can adapt each other's ideas rather than having to plan each lesson from scratch.

We would recommend, however, that whatever style or layout of lesson planning you choose, you try to include a few key elements, listed below.

- *Who the class is aimed at and roughly how many you are expecting?* Obviously, these two basic facts impact on every element of your lesson. It's worth having this as a reminder when you are planning your lesson, but also for when you are casting around for ideas in future (or sharing ideas with colleagues). Old lesson plans well labelled with who and how many they were aimed at make it easy to see where you can adapt and recycle ideas.

- *The objectives of the session.* You should also have a broad 'aim' behind the session that helps you to set the objectives, but it isn't always necessary to list this on the plan. As a minimum, however, make sure the objectives are clearly listed in terms of what you wish the students to know, or be able to do, not in terms of what you want to do in the session. A good objective is therefore likely to start with a phrase like '*At the end of this session, learners will be able to …*'

- *Don't have too many objectives.* You need to keep them relevant to the overall aim of the session and easy for you to assess if they have been achieved.

- *Timings.* These only need to be approximate, but they show you the flow of the session and help you adapt while you are teaching so you don't either run out of time or finish unnecessarily early. Remember while you plan the timings that the average attention span is less than ten minutes, so try to plan a change of pace or activity every ten minutes if possible to keep your learners fresh and focussed. Don't forget to include timings for breaks, introductions and settling in, and for questions and to review knowledge.

- *Activities you'll be carrying out and the objectives these will meet.* These two should be linked so you'll always know if you're covering your planned objectives. If activities don't seem to meet your objectives, then think whether you need them as part of the session. Make sure you include as activities some way of 'setting the scene' at the start of the session, so learners know what is expected in the class, along with a way of summarising what has been learnt in the session, which may be combined with assessing learning (see below).

- *How each objective will be assessed.* You can plan an impressive sounding session, with fantastic objectives, exciting, creative activities and great supporting materials, but if you don't know if anyone has met any of the learning objectives you have set then what was the point? You should make sure that you assess all of your learning objectives during the session. This may be as simple as a show of hands or feeding back a quick discussion to you and the whole class, but you need to plan for this assessment from the start.

■ *Materials and equipment needed.* It helps if this is pulled together into one place and easy to check off so you know you have everything you need before you go into a session.

■ *Other elements.* Think about other elements that may be particularly useful to you in your situation, and include these in every plan. This may be how you provide differentiation between learners in the class (so there are elements for everyone), or what information literacy competencies you are covering with each activity. Have confidence to include elements that work for you and adapt your template accordingly.

Blank lesson plan templates

Lesson plan template 1

Title of Lesson:

Date/Time:

Venue:

Level:

Class Size:

Aim of Lesson:

Learning Objectives of lesson: Learners will be able to … .

Handouts/equipment required:

Timings (approx.)	Activity (aim for change of activity at least every 10 minutes)	Objective (to match objectives listed above)	Notes

Lesson plan template 2

Information Skills Plan

Date: Time: Venue:

Course: No. of students:

Handouts required:
☐ ☐ ☐

TOPIC:

OUTCOMES:
Learners will be able to: [use verbs which indicate a concrete, assessable result]
√ Explain …
√ Identify …
√ List …

Time:	Teacher activity	Learner activity	Resource	Assessment	Info. Literacy Skill
	Introduction				
	Conclusion				

Citation searching and impact factors

Techniques used from this book: Buzz groups, Go to your post.

Target audience: Researchers and academic staff.

Maximum class size: Preferably small, perhaps 10 or 12 at most.

Expected outcomes: Learners will be able to:

- Express the advantages and limitations of citation searching.
- Carry out a citation search using both Google Scholar and Web of Science.
- Calculate the h-index and impact factor for an article.
- Find the impact factor of a journal using the Journal Citation Reports.
- Select the highest ranking journal in their subject area using the Journal Citation Reports.

Time: 60 minutes.

Handouts required: Summary of main points covered (to be given out at the end of the session).

Equipment required: Computer per person. Access to Web of Science and Journal Citation Reports. Sticky note or piece of paper containing title and year of each article used in the first exercise.

Outline of session:

0–5 minutes: Introduction to session. Outline what will be covered in the session, including the expected outcomes. Explain why these outcomes will be important to them. Ask a series of questions related to the learning outcomes to assess the confidence level of the class. Use one wall of the classroom to denote 'Very confident'; one side to denote 'What on earth is that!', the middle to denote 'Not very confident'. Example questions could be: 'How confident are you that you could find the impact factor of a journal?', 'How confident would you be in carrying out a citation search?' *Introduction and setting the scene.*

6–10 minutes: Give an example of a journal article with a large list of references that has been cited several times by other articles. Some of the citing articles should themselves have been cited by others. Put a sticky note or piece of paper on the wall containing the title and year of the sample article. Give the articles referenced by that article (again on sticky notes or small pieces of paper) and ask a member of the class to stick them all to the left of the original article. Ask someone else to stick the 'cited by' sticky notes to the right of the article, then a third person to stick the next level of 'cited by' notes up. Use this series of sticky notes to explain how citation searching moves through the web they have created. *Objective – express the advantages and limitations of citation searching.*

11–15 minutes: Ask the class to pair up and spend two minutes discussing citation searching, its advantages and the reasons it may not be useful. Ask one group at a time to feedback one of their points to the whole class. Fill in any gaps yourself at the end. *Objective – express the advantages and limitations of citation searching.*

16–20 minutes: Use the web of references to explain how the impact factor and h-index of the central article may be calculated. Ask a member of the class to actually work each of them out. *Objectives – express the advantages and limitations of citation searching, calculate the h-index and impact factor for an article.*

21–25 minutes: Demonstrate how to access Web of Science and Google Scholar, including an explanation of what they are. Carry out a citation search in each of these using a different article in each. *Objective – carry out a citation search using both Google Scholar and Web of Science.*

26–35 minutes: Get the class to log on to the computers and carry out a citation search using a reference you provide in both Google Scholar and Web of Science. Choose an article that gives different numbers of citing articles in each resource. Again, get the class to pair up and discuss why this may be so. Ask for explanations from the pairs. *Objective – carry out a citation search using both Google Scholar and Web of Science.*

36–40 minutes: Demonstrate Journal Citation Reports, explaining what the resource is and why it may be of interest to them. *Objectives – find the impact factor of a journal using the Journal Citation Reports, select the highest ranking journal in their subject area using the Journal Citation Reports.*

41–50 minutes: Set the class (as individuals) to find the impact factor of a journal (named by you) and to find the highest ranking journal in 'their' subject area. *Objectives – find the impact factor of a journal using the*

Journal Citation Reports, select the highest ranking journal in their subject area using the *Journal Citation Reports.*

51–55 minutes: Sum up the session and ask for questions.

56–60 minutes: Ask the same questions as at the start to check that confidence levels have increased.

Note: Assessment is integrated into the activities.

Current awareness made easy

Techniques used from this book: Any improvements?; Quick vote.

Target audience: Anyone who needs to keep up to date with a topic area such as health professionals, legal professionals, researchers and advanced higher education students.

Maximum class size: Depends on size of the largest computer lab you have access to. If the class is larger than around 12 we would recommend having two instructors to ensure class members have enough one-to-one help.

Expected outcomes: Learners will be able to:

- Set up email alerts from a database of their choice.
- Set up and use an RSS reader.
- Find RSS feeds from journals and others sources of interest and set them up in an RSS reader.
- Set up search alerts in a database of interest.

Time: 60 minutes.

Handouts required: Sample handout given below – this guides the learners through an exercise as well as acting as future reference.

Equipment required: At least one computer between every two learners. one piece of A5 or A6 card for each member of the class.

Outline of session:

0–5 minutes: Introduction to session. Outline what will be covered in the session, including the expected outcomes. Explain why these outcomes will be important to them.

   If this is one session in a series of classes, include a quick look back at the last session, preferably including a check of knowledge based on the outcomes of the previous session. *Introduction and setting the scene.*

6–10 minutes: Quick vote – ask the class how many people are currently trying to keep up to date with their subject area (hopefully for professionals from any sector, as well as researchers, this should be a decent percentage!). Ask them to spend two minutes working out roughly how much time they may spend each week keeping up to date in their subject area and write the number of minutes down on a piece of card (without showing anyone else). When they've done this, they should pass the cards to the front of the class.

11–20 minutes: Show (with a database appropriate to your audience) how to carry out a search and set up an email search alert that will update at set periods. Ask everyone to do this themselves for a topic of interest to them. This is your opportunity to make sure that everyone in the class can access your electronic resources – make sure you wander around the whole class and see everyone access a database. This is why we would recommend the ratio of instructors to learners is not much more than 1:12. *Objective – set up email alerts from a database of choice.*

21–25 minutes: Show a picture of the typical orange RSS icon on screen. Ask how many recognise it. Explain briefly what Really Simple Syndication (RSS) is – if you think you'll struggle to do this, there are plenty of YouTube videos that could do it for you. Ask how many people currently use RSS feeds and how many use an RSS reader. Show examples of one or two RSS readers including content at the front of the class. *Objective – set up and use an RSS reader.*

25–50 minutes: Exercise – example given below. This should talk them through setting up an RSS reader (though they can use their own if they already have one) and finding RSS feeds from various sources. Again, make sure you move around the class helping where necessary and keeping them on task. Also during the exercise, collate the cards they passed to the front at the start of the session so you know how long people said they spent on current awareness each week. Total this and put it into a quick chart on the instructor's PC, but don't make it visible to the class. *Objectives – set up and use an RSS reader, find RSS feeds from journals and others sources of interest and set them up in an RSS reader.*

50–55 minutes: Ask for any questions or problems that you haven't addressed during the exercise.

55–60 minutes: Ask the class again, one person at a time, how long they think they'll need to spend in current awareness now they know about email and RSS alerts. Put this into the chart as you work around the class. Display the 'before' and 'after' figures to the whole class. Hopefully you'll be able to show an overall time saving! If you have access to interactive handsets (sometimes called clickers), collecting this information at the start and end of the session is a great use for them. *Summarising the session and assessment.*

Note: Most assessment is integrated into the activities, which is why you need to circulate and check the class are successful with the activities.

Example worksheet: Current awareness made easy.

Activity will involve:

- Setting up an RSS Reader using Bloglines
- Setting up an RSS feed from the *Financial Times* website
- Setting up an RSS feed from an online journal
- Using ticTOCs to find Table of Contents from journals.

Bloglines is just one freely available web-based RSS Reader. It has been chosen for this activity purely because it is simple to use, free and accessible from any computer with an internet connection. Bloglines offers many more functions beyond reading RSS feeds which you may wish to explore at another time.

RSS stands for 'Really Simply Syndication', most commonly shown by (normally coloured orange), though there are many variations on this simple logo. It allows websites and producers of information to easily make their updated content available in a format that can be viewed in a range of different programs, often referred to as RSS readers.

They are an easy way for us to pull new content from a range of sources, including websites and online journals, into one place so we can see the latest updates.

Setting up an RSS Reader using Bloglines:

- Go to *http://www.bloglines.com/*.
- You may like to find out more about this service by clicking 'About' at the bottom of the screen and choosing 'Frequently Asked Questions'. If not, click "Sign up now, it's free!"
- Fill in your details, choose a password and click.
- You will need to check your email to confirm your registration to proceed.
- Bloglines will suggest some subscriptions for you. Feel free to choose some or ignore.
- Choose the tab.
- This is where your RSS feeds will appear. You can add, edit, delete feeds and create folders.
- Leave this window open for the following exercises.

Setting up an RSS feed from the *Financial Times* website:

- Open a new window.
- Go to *http://www.ft.com/home/uk*.
- Look for the RSS logo on this page and click on it.

Pick which RSS feed reflects the news you are interested in and click on it. Then simply copy the web address from the address bar.

- Go back to the window with Bloglines open and choose Add.

Paste the address into the box ...and click Subscribe.

- The next page will simply confirm the details of the feed. Click Subscribe again to see your feed!
- Leave this window open.

Setting up an RSS feed from an online journal: This exercise will show you an example of how to set up an RSS feed from an e-journal. Not all e-journals provide RSS feeds, and the process may vary slightly between journals.

- Open a new window.
- Go to *http://hbr.harvardbusiness.org/* – the homepage for the journal *Harvard Business Review*.
- Look at the bottom of the screen for the RSS feeds link and click on it.
- Again, copy the web address from the address bar.
- Go back to the window with Bloglines open and choose Add.

Paste the address into the box ...and click Subscribe.

- Again, the next page will simply confirm the details of the feed. Click subscribe again to see your feed!
- This will 'feed' the Table of Contents of this journal to Bloglines every time a new article becomes available.
- The easiest way to find RSS feeds for journals is often from the publisher's website.

Using ticTOCs to automatically pull tables of contents into an RSS feed: An alternative to visiting publishers' websites is to use a service like ticTOCs, that pulls the table of contents pages from lots of journals into one place.

- Visit *http://www.tictocs.ac.uk/*.
- Use the search box on the left-hand side to either search for individual journals of interest or by subject area. Browsing by subject area can often be the best way to find journals.

- When you find a journal that looks interesting either click on the orange RSS icon and follow the instructions in the previous activities to copy it to Bloglines, or click on 'Add to MyTOCSs'.

- If you choose 'Add to MyTOCs', they will be listed down the right hand side of the screen.

- If you register with ticTOCs, then this list will be saved and you can view it each time you log into the service. New items will appear in bold.

Setting up an RSS feed to update a search in a database: Some databases let you set up RSS feeds for search results.

- Go to metalib (the resource used at the University of Huddersfield at the time of writing!).

- Find Business Source Premier (Under Business & Law, Journals).

- Conduct a search, e.g. retail change management.

- You will see a list of results.

- Click on the orange icon at the top of the list of results.

- This will give you the option to set up an RSS feed or an email alert. To use the email service you would need to register.

- Right click on the complicated looking URL and choose 'copy shortcut'.

- Then click on Save alert.

- Go back to the window with Bloglines open and choose Add.

Paste the address into the box ... and click Subscribe.

- Again, the next page will simply confirm the details of the feed. Click subscribe again to see your feed!

- Every time new articles match your search you will receive the details in Bloglines.

You might now like to:

- Check your Bloglines account again to see what's new.

- Set up more feeds from different websites, journals, library catalogues, news sites, blogs.

- Find out whether your frequently used journals or databases facilitate RSS feeds.

- Investigate some of the alternative RSS readers below.

A few alternative RSS readers:

Google Reader – *http://www.google.com/reader/view/*

Feedbucket – *http://www.feedbucket.com/*

Netvibes – *http://www.netvibes.com*

Evaluating web resources

Techniques used from this book: I resolve to; Poster tours.

Target audience: Schools, public, FE, HE.

Maximum class size: Depends on size of largest computer room you have available.

Expected outcomes: Learners will be able to:

- Evaluate the information quality of websites.

Time: 60 minutes.

Handouts required:

- Checklist for evaluating websites. Include on this at least one of the freely available online tutorials as a way of students revising the session.

Equipment required: One computer between two people. Piece of A5 card per person. Piece of flipchart paper between two people. Assortment of pens for flipchart paper.

Outline of session:

0–5 minutes: Introduction to session. Outline what will be covered in the session, including the expected outcomes. Explain why these outcomes will be important to them. *Introduction and setting the scene.*

6–15 minutes: Explain that when we are looking for information on the internet not all web pages are of equal quality and it can be hard to work out which to trust. Show a series of web pages, some genuine, trustworthy sites, others spoof or 'dubious science' sites (those selling pseudo-scientific gadgets can be quite good examples). Phil Bradley has a list of useful sites (*http://www.philb.com/fakesites.htm*) though some of these are starting to look a little dated. Make sure you check any suggested sites out before the class starts to ensure they are suitable for the age group you are teaching. As you show each web page, ask for comments from the class as to why it may or may not be a site you can rely on for quality information. Pull together a list of reasons to trust or distrust each site at the front of the class. *Objective – evaluate the information quality of websites.*

16–20 minutes: Give out your pre-prepared checklist for evaluating websites. Highlight to the class some of the key issues that may not have been raised already. Split the class into pairs.

20–45 minutes: Ask each group to carry out an internet search on a topic of interest to them or that they are covering in other classes, and pick three resources. They should evaluate each of these resources and write on flipchart paper a summary of each site and their findings. *Objective – evaluate the information quality of websites.*

46–55 minutes: For a small class size, the flipchart paper should be stuck on the walls of the classroom and each pair should work their way around the room looking at each group's results and adding comments using a different coloured pen. You should shout or blow a whistle when it is time to move on to the next poster. For large groups, split the class into several groups of the original pairings and carry out the same exercise but passing the posters from pair to pair within the larger grouping. *Objectives – evaluate the information quality of websites. Assessment takes place here.*

56–60 minutes: Sum up, deal with any questions and address quickly any deficiencies you may have spotted during the exercise. Then give out a piece of A5 card per person. Ask them to write how the session will change the way they search for and use information on the internet in future, write their names (and contact details if necessary) and pass the cards to the front of the class. *Summarising the session and assessment.*

After the class: One month later, send the cards back out to the class members with a note asking them if their behaviour really has changed in the way they expected.

The information cycle

Techniques used from this book: The model literature review; Sharing results by wiki.

Target audience: School age or college students.

Maximum class size: around 30.

Expected outcomes: Learners will be able to:

- Identify and express the characteristics of, and timescales involved in, different resources through the information cycle.

Time: 60 minutes.

Handouts required: A wiki with pages for each type of media you want the group to consider. Set of instructions (and usernames and passwords if needed) on editing your chosen wiki. Set of descriptions of fictional event (see partial examples given later).

Equipment required: Pots of modelling clay. One computer per group. Digital camera (at least one, but more would make the logistics of sharing easier!).

Outline of session:

0–5 minutes: Introduction to session. Outline what will be covered in the session, including the expected outcomes. Explain why these outcomes will be important to them. *Introduction and setting the scene.*

6–10 minutes: Briefly explain that after a newsworthy event, information is reported in a range of different media from the 'quick and dirty' online social media such as Twitter, to the slow, considered production of print encyclopaedia entries years later. Split them into small groups and allocate each group a type of media. Give each group a handout describing a fictitious event, with reporting from a different type of media for each group. (Examples of two information sources are given below.) *Objectives – identify and express the characteristics of, and timescales involved in, different resources through the information cycle.*

11–15 minutes: Give each group five minutes to look at the example materials.

16–20 minutes: Give each group a pot of modelling clay and ask every member of each group to spend 60 seconds creating a model that represents the media they've been given. They then have to spend up to a minute describing their model and the attributes they feel fits their group's type of media. *Objectives – identify and express the characteristics of, and timescales involved in, different resources through the information cycle.*

21–40 minutes: After the individual descriptions, they should then agree as a group a list of attributes describing their group's type of media. One person should enter that list into a page on a pre-prepared wiki you've created, while the other members use the modelling clay to create a group representation of the media. They should then take a photo of the model to use at the top of their wiki page. *Objectives – identify and express the characteristics of, and timescales involved in, different resources through the information cycle.*

41–50 minutes: The groups should report back to the whole class on the attributes of their media by showing the page they have created. Comments and discussion should be encouraged and any major omissions or errors can be corrected during each short report. *Objectives – identify and express the characteristics of, and timescales involved in, different resources through the information cycle. Assessment takes place here.*

50–55 minutes: Point out that the different characteristics of the types of media make them suitable for different uses. Do a quick quiz by listing some uses for information and asking them to vote for the most appropriate source. *Objectives – identify and express the characteristics of, and timescales involved in, different resources through the information cycle. Assessment takes place here, along with summarising the session.*

56–60 minutes: Opportunity for them to ask any questions. Encourage them to go back on a later date to comment on each other's wiki pages and point out any further resources on the information cycle that you will have linked to from the front page of the wiki.

Example handouts/material:

Overall story summary: An experiment by a local inventor has gone wrong. In an attempt to reduce the damage caused by rabbits to vegetable plots in the area, it's believed he has not only transferred aspects of his own brain function and personality onto a rabbit, he has also transformed himself into a giant rabbit-like creature that causes massive damage whenever the full moon triggers the transformation.

This example is based on the plot of Wallace & Gromit: The Curse of the Were-Rabbit *by Aardman Animations limited. Pick your own fictional story, or use examples from real stories.*

Handouts follow for Twitter and Academic Journals.

Twitter pack:

@vegmad, 10:05: Something dodgy's been going on, whole garden looks like a bombsite!!!

@carrot123, 10:09: Me too, @vegmad – only my veg plot though, nothings touched the decking.

@vegmad, 10:10: @carrot123 Just my veg as well – but trashed the garden, heard a right racket a few mins ago but it'd gone before I could see what caused it.

@cabbagelover, 10:15: Something massive in the garden just now – my wife's brassicas will never be the same again. #vegmonster.

@peasforall, 10:16: What was that! Some sort of bear just gone past my window!!!

@vegmad, 10:16: RT @peasforall: What was that! Some sort of bear just gone past my window!!! #vegmonster.

@carrot123, 10:18: @vegmad @peasforall Bears? In England? Trashing veg gardens??? #vegmonster.

@vegmad, 10:19: @peasforall can you get a better look? #vegmonster.

@peasforall, 10:21: Nice and clear oustide (full moon tonight), but it's gone out of sight already. Massive footprint though. #vegmonster.

@conspiracy666, 10:21: Heard rumours about some sort of kerfuffle in gardens tonight – I told you all GM crops were dangerous. #vegmonster #gmcrops.

@Potatoeshaveeyes, 10:22: Out in the garden and some sort of big fluffy creature with enormous ears just jumped over me. Not drinking any more tonight.

@peasforall, 10:24: RT @Potatoeshaveeyes: Out in the garden and some sort of big fluffy creature with enormous ears just jumped over me. Not drinking any more tonight. #vegmonster.

@peasforall, 10:24: Is it some sort of escaped zoo creature then? Or aliens? #vegmonster.

@carrot123, 10:26: No, it'll be some crackpot device from that local inventor again I bet! I'm sure I saw his do out and about. #vegmonster #gmadinventor.

@farmerg, 10:26: @conspiracy666: Nonsense – it'll be all that organic stuff. Not good spreading all that muck on gardens I tell you! #vegmonster #madorganics.

@potatoeshaveeyes, 10:28: I can't still be seeing things – it looks like some sort of massive rabbit eating the neighbours veg. Clear as a bell in this full moon.

@prettygirls, 10:29: Have you seen my new pictures? Visit soon! #vegmonster.

@carrot123, 10:30: @potatoeshaveeyes No, it's not just you – there's something dodgy going on tonight. Sister says it's a monster kangaroo. #vegmonster.

Peer reviewed journal articles:

Ventor (2009)

Abstract: In this article we investigate the influence of the lunar cycle to amplify the effectiveness of the transfer of human/rodent brain pattern. Particular attention is paid to the practicalities of trapping and utilising the light during a full moon to increase the effect. This paper is the first to build on the recent Lancastrian work in the context of the more traditional wolf based Eastern European tradition.

Roger et al. (2009)

Abstract: Garden tools such as spades, hoes, sickles and scythes have been the gardeners friends for thousands of years against weeds and common garden pests such as slugs and snails. However, it is a large step between chopping a slug in half with a spade and dealing with an eight foot tall monster. This paper looks at the adaptability of everyday tools to deal with larger pests in the light of a recent monster rabbit infestation. It recommends those tools most adaptable for use by angry mobs and suggests minor improvements for garden suppliers to ensure their tools are suitable for both purposes.

References

Roger, A., Wilco, B. and Out, C. (2009) 'Gardening implements or mob supplies: the adaptability of everyday tools in the fight to protect against more than slugs and snails', *Horticultural Implement Research*, 28 (4): 241–50.

Ventor, M. (2009) 'Human to rodent brain transfer: a lunar amplified approach', *International Journal of Rodent Human Studies*, 12 (3): 123–35.

Introducing Dewey

Techniques used from this book: ... And now for the news; Go to your post.

Target audience: School aged children – for school or public librarians.

Maximum class size: Around 30.

Expected outcomes: Learners will be able to:

- Recognise and explain to others how a classification scheme works.
- Use Dewey to find materials in your library (or other preferred classification scheme).

Time: 90 minutes.

Handouts required: How to upload a video to YouTube. Brief guide to Dewey.

Equipment required: A digital video camera per group. A computer (fixed or laptop) per group connected to the internet. Access to the library. Assortment of books on a range of topics. YouTube Account.

Outline of session:

0–5 minutes: Introduction to session. Outline what will be covered in the session, including the expected outcomes. Explain why these outcomes will be important to them. *Introduction and setting the scene.*

6–15 minutes: Split the class into either three or six or nine groups (depending on size of the class – no more than about five in a group). Give each of them a trolley part full of books on a range of topics and ask them to organise them into groups that would make it easy for someone else to find them in a library. They need to write down a short list of rules that decide what book goes in each grouping. *Objective – recognise and explain to others how a classification scheme works.*

16–20 minutes: The groups should take turns to explain their groupings and associated rules to the whole class. *Objectives – recognise and explain to others how a classification scheme works. Assessment takes place here.*

21–25 minutes: Explain to them that they have designed their own classification scheme. Show them how Dewey works and give them a handout as reference. Explain the layout of your own library with respect to Dewey. *Objectives – recognise and explain to others how a classification scheme works, use Dewey (or other preferred classification scheme) to find materials in your library.*

26–60 minutes: Give each group a video camera and explain that you want them to produce a video explaining to others: (1) What a classification scheme is, (2) how Dewey is organised or (3) how to use Dewey to find books in your library. Assign the videos evenly through the class (the reason for having three, six or nine groups). Give them a deadline of 30 minutes to research, write a script and agree parts for the video, then five minutes to shoot it at the end. All videos must be recorded in one continuous shoot (no editing). *Objectives – recognise and explain to others how a classification scheme works, use Dewey (or other preferred classification scheme) to find materials in your library.*

60–65 minutes: The groups should upload their videos to YouTube, using a free account you should have set up previously. If your school or library blocks access to YouTube, upload it to another online resource, such as a free blog service (that will still allow you to post comments on each video and view externally), or on your own servers.

66–85 minutes: The groups should view each other's videos and leave comments on them. You may need to give guidance on the sort of comments you want to see – for instance, 'How useful was this video?', 'How well did it explain the objective it was set?', 'How would you improve the explanation on the video?'. *Objectives – recognise and explain to others how a classification scheme works, use Dewey (or other preferred classification scheme) to find materials in your library. Assessment takes place here.*

86–90 minutes: Sum up at the end and check knowledge with a few True and False questions – read out a statement about Dewey and using it to find items and ask them to go to one side of the classroom if they think the statement is True, the other side if they think the statement is False. Finish by reminding them they can view their videos and carry on posting statements afterwards if they wish. *Summarising and assessment.*

Referencing and plagiarism

Techniques used from this book: Poster tours; Washing line search strategy.

Target audience: Mainly 16+ students.

Maximum class size: Around 20.

Expected outcomes: Learners will be able to:

- Express what plagiarism is and why it is important to avoid.
- Use the preferred referencing style in your institution for common types of information sources.

Time: 60 minutes.

Handouts required: A guide to your institution's preferred referencing style.

Equipment required: At least one computer between two members of the class. Length of string and set of small pegs per group of three or four students. Set of cards for each group of three or four students, comprising the main components of a reference to an item. A description (or copy in the case of a print item) of the item you want each group to construct a reference for. Sticky tack for each group. Flip chart and paper.

Outline of session:

0–5 minutes: Introduction to session. Outline what will be covered in the session, including the expected outcomes. Explain why these outcomes will be important to them. *Introduction and setting the scene.*

6–10 minutes: It is likely that their teachers or lecturers would have mentioned plagiarism already, so ask the class to discuss in pairs what they think plagiarism is, for two minutes. Work round the class asking for their thoughts and writing these down on a flip chart. Discuss their results – you may need to point out some of the less obvious ways of plagiarising another's work. *Objectives – express what plagiarism is and why it is important to avoid. Assessment takes place here.*

11–20 minutes: Ask them to try a short online tutorial on plagiarism. A good one is by the Vaughan Memorial Library (*http://library.acadiau.ca/ tutorials/plagiarism/*), which should take 10 minutes, but there are many different options freely available on the internet – as long as you credit them in class of course! *Objective – express what plagiarism is and why it is important to avoid.*

21–30 minutes: Ask if they have any questions on what is, or isn't, plagiarism. Explain that once they know *what* they need to reference, next they need to know *how* to reference correctly. Ask them to try the first set of activities in the Liberation Referencing online tutorial (*http://library.northampton.ac.uk/liberation/ref/cat.php*) produced by the library at the University of Northampton. This uses the Harvard referencing system, but concentrates on how you may find the right information from a book to construct your reference, so can be applied to other referencing systems. It is a fantastic resource, which uses a cartoon cat to illustrate how well you do in the exercises. *Objectives – express what plagiarism is and why it is important to avoid, use the preferred referencing style in your institution for common types of information sources.*

31–40 minutes: Give out your institution's approved referencing guides and split the class into groups of three or four. Give each group an item to reference, a length of string, a set of small pegs, and cards made up of the components of the reference for the item you want them to reference. Each group needs a different item to reference, covering the types of information resources you want to cover in your session. Ask them to construct a correct reference using the cards, string and pegs. When completed, they should stick the string containing the correct reference to a patch of wall using sticky tack, next to the item they are referencing. You should put a piece of flip chart paper next to each reference. *Objectives – use the preferred referencing style in your institution for common types of information sources. Assessment takes place here.*

41–50 minutes: Each group stands next to their reference and then moves clockwise around the room to look at the next group's reference. They should check the reference using their guides and either put a tick on the flip chart paper next to it or write what they feel is the correct reference. The amount of time you give each group depends on how much time you have left at this stage and the number of group you have, but make sure they get to look at every reference. *Objectives – use the preferred referencing style in your institution for common types of information sources. Assessment takes place here.*

51–55 minutes: Quickly run through each reference to correct any mistakes and discuss disagreements (if applicable). *Summarise and assessment.*

56–60 minutes: Ask for any questions and signpost further sources of information. The rest of the Liberation Referencing tutorial used above is worth recommending, along with any resources you may have on your own website. *Summarise the session and look forward to future learning.*

Search smarter, search faster

Techniques used from this book: All stand; Buzz groups; I will do it; Stop, start, continue.

Target audience: Anyone who may need to improve their generic search skills. Example given here is for Higher Education, but can easily be adapted by switching the databases searched with other appropriate resources – so in a UK law firm the examples could be legal resources such as BIALLI or the OPSI site, or for US public libraries it could include searching freely available State and National Government sites (to improve digital citizenship), or for school age children resources such as video and picture sharing sites they may find useful when putting work together for assignments.

Maximum class size: unlimited.

Expected outcomes: Learners will be able to:

■ Use truncation; wildcards and Boolean operators to search Google Scholar and Business Source Premier.

■ Be able to explain why they may save time and effort using these search techniques.

Time: 90 minutes.

Handouts required: General search tips to take away (set of basic search tips, including links to videos used). Google Tips sheet (*www.google. com/librariancenter/downloads/Tips_Tricks_85x11.pdf*). Exercise sheet (for use in class – to try search techniques in resources appropriate to your students).

Equipment required: Projector with sound. Internet connection. Enough computers for one between two OR the same number of computers available nearby (so the class can be sent away for computer based exercise). Sticky notes.

Outline of session:

0–5 minutes: Introduction to session. Outline what will be covered in the session, including the expected outcomes. Explain why these outcomes will be important to them. *Introduction and setting the scene.*

6–15 minutes: As an introduction to the concept of advanced search techniques, show the class the YouTube video entitled 'Search Smarter,

Search Faster' (*www.youtube.com/watch?v=Oa66AxTbjxA*) produced by the library at the University of Sydney (uniofsydney is their YouTube name) and available in alternative formats from their webpages (*http://www.library.usyd.edu.au/skills/*). This video covers concepts such as 'constructing a search strategy', 'Finding synonyms for search terms' and 'Boolean Operators'. *Objectives – use truncation; wildcards and Boolean operators to search Google Scholar, Business Source Premier.*

16–25 minutes: Talk to the class about the idea of a search strategy. The video shows one way of constructing a search strategy, but another popular way of exploring concepts to lead to an improved search strategy is mind maps. Explain what a mind map is and show them a graphical representation of one on screen. Point them towards resources they may find useful if they wish to investigate them in future. Ask the class to split into pairs and spend five minutes discussing how familiar the concepts are of constructing search strategies and finding synonyms (the first two areas covered by the video). Ask them to consider as pairs where they might be useful and how they might find search terms for the topics they are interested in. *Objectives – be able to explain why they may save time and effort using these search techniques.*

26–30 minutes: If the class is large (perhaps over 20), get the pairs to combine into fours; then eights (if necessary), sharing the results of their discussions with the larger groups for two minutes at a time. This will make it easier to feedback to the front. Ask the groups to share their discussions with the whole class. Hopefully there will be a general consensus that these ideas will save them time and make it easier to search for information. If no-one mentions it, tell them yourself that an important area to look for synonyms is where there are differences in American and UK English. You should be able to assess how well the class have understood these ideas from their feedback. If necessary explain briefly anything they don't seem to have fully understood and if necessary signpost them towards further resources and activities. *Objectives – be able to explain why they may save time and effort using these search techniques.*

31–35 minutes: Do a quick 'active' exercise to check if people understand ideas behind Boolean operators (the third area covered by the video). The exact way you do this will depend on the size of room and number of students you have, but the easiest way for a class of any size is to ask everyone to stand up. Then call out different combinations of students using the operators AND and OR (and NOT if you wish) using the students' physical characteristics or that of their clothing and ask only those who meet the search to stay standing. For example, 'People who are male AND have short hair stay standing', 'People who wear glasses OR are female stay standing'. After four or five combinations you should be able to judge if they understand the main Boolean operators. *Objectives – use truncation, wildcards and Boolean operators to search Google Scholar, Business Source Premier. Assessment takes place here.*

36–40 minutes: For more explanation of Boolean searching, try watching the librarian Goose video on this topic (Boolean searching video *www.youtube.com/watch?v=enPSOq1_QmY* by Gareth Johnson – Youtube name Lordllama), including a short discussion at the end to once again check understanding. This video and discussion can be missed out if you think they fully understand the concept after the previous exercise. *Objectives – use truncation; wildcards and Boolean operators to search Google Scholar, Business Source Premier. Be able to explain why they may save time and effort using these search techniques.*

41–45 minutes: Show YouTube video *www.youtube.com/watch?v=Jf_gEM4lohc* by Edinburgh Napier University Library (YouTube name EdNapLib) on truncation and wildcards. *Objectives – use truncation, wildcards and Boolean operators to search Google Scholar, Business Source Premier.*

46–55 minutes: Show on screen the different forms of wildcards and how they might be used combined with how Boolean searching works. Demonstrate using at least two online resources, preferably a generic one such as Google and a more specialised one (if appropriate) that may use slightly different wildcards.

Start with a question, split it into the concepts you may wish to search for, talk about what synonyms you may wish to use and show on screen the search strategy developing. Then use this search strategy to demonstrate the ideas described above. After this demonstration give the class their handouts. *Objectives – use truncation, wildcards and Boolean operators to search Google Scholar, Business Source Premier.*

56–75 minutes: Class exercise – 'using advanced search techniques to search a range of resources'. *Objectives – use truncation, wildcards and Boolean operators to search Google Scholar, Business Source Premier. Assessment takes place here.*

76–80 minutes: Discussion/give answers to exercise sheet.

81–85 minutes: Summarise what you've covered in the class and ask students to write down three things from the session that they've learnt and will use in future. *Summarise the session.*

86–90 minutes: If the session is part of a series, quickly look forward to what topics will be covered in the next session. Ask the class for feedback via sticky notes (preferably giant sized ones if available) – tell them to write down STOP plus what they didn't like about the session, START plus whatever they'd like to have been included but wasn't, and CONTINUE plus what they liked best about the session. They should put these sticky notes on the wall as they leave the session. *Assess the content and delivery of your session.*

Types of information resources

Techniques used from this book: Buzz groups; I resolve to; Quick vote; Runaround.

Target audience: Mainly higher education students, particularly under graduates who may not have explored the range of information sources available. It can be adapted to any group of learners who have typically relied on a narrow range of information resources.

Maximum class size: No limit, but the larger the number of students the more time consuming and awkward the feedback to the front will be.

Expected outcomes: Learners will be able to:

■ Identify a wide range of information sources.

■ Describe the most appropriate type of information resources for different types of activity.

Time: 45 minutes.

Handouts required: Sheet describing a range of information resources and their key attributes.

Equipment required: A4 pieces of card with a type of information source typed at the top. Include the open web, text books, print encyclopaedia, academic journals, newspapers and any others that may be appropriate to your group. A piece of A5 card each.

Outline of session:

0–5 minutes: Introduction to session. Outline what will be covered in the session, including the expected outcomes. Explain why these outcomes will be important to them. *Introduction and setting the scene.*

6–10 minutes: Get the class to vote on how many people use different information sources for their studies – start with the open web/wikipedia, then text books, journal articles, then ask if they use any other sources of information. This should give you an idea of the range of resources currently being used. Explain there is a wide range of different types of information sources that they can use beyond this small set. *Objectives – identify a wide range of information sources.*

11–15 minutes: Split them into groups of three or four people. Give them two minutes to write down a list of as many different sources of information as they can think of. Work your way around the class asking each group to name one source of information, continuing until the groups run out of ideas. Tally up the ideas as they come, so at the end you can say how many they could think of. Display a long list of different sources of information on screen – you should be able to think of a considerable list to fill the screen with fairly small sized text. Explain that this illustrates the massive range of types of information that are available, but that you will concentrate on just a handful today. *Objectives – identify a wide range of information sources.*

16–25 minutes: Pass around the A4 pieces of card that have a type of information sources printed at the top, one per group. Make sure you hand out the ones you feel are most important for your group. You should aim to have more of these cards prepared in advance than you think you'll need. Ask them, as groups, to write down the attributes of their information sources. As an example display on the screen at the front some important attributes of a text book (such as: 'slow to publish – one to two years', 'may give good overview of a topic', 'can vary significantly in quality', 'textbooks are likely to give further references to follow', etc.). In addition you may want to provide them with a list of qualities to consider (currency, bias, academic level, etc.). After around five minutes, ask them to finish and come to the front, one group at a time, to describe the attributes of 'their' resources. This is also an opportunity for the class as a whole to say if they agree or disagree with the attributes. You may also need to add some important attributes to the resources at this stage. *Objectives – identify a wide range of information sources, describe the most appropriate type of information resources for different types of activity. Assessment takes place here.*

25–35 minutes: If there is sufficient space in the classroom, stick each of the pieces of cards around the walls of the class. Explain that you are going to describe a need for information and you want everyone to go to the information resource (i.e. the card) most appropriate to meet that need. Put on the screen at the front an information need (for example, 'starting out on a completely new topic', or 'finding the latest research on a topic') and tell them they have 30 seconds to go to the most appropriate resource. Once there, give them a few seconds (depending on size of room and space!) opportunity to change their mind – it can be nice to use a countdown timer and dramatic music using an interactive whiteboard application, or one freely available from the internet. Those standing near the 'wrong' resource should be told to sit down. Continue until you've given an information need appropriate to each information source. Once finished, it can be a nice idea to give a small prize, such as a small bar of chocolate to each person still standing. *Objectives – describe the most appropriate type of information resources for different types of activity. Assessment takes place here.*

36–40 minutes: Explain how they've seen that there are a wide range of information sources appropriate to different needs and summarise some of the key information sources and their attributes. Ask if they've any questions they'd like to ask. *Summarise the session.*

41–45 minutes: Give them all a piece of A5 card. Ask them to write their email address (this can be optional if you wish) on the card, along with how they plan to use the information they've learnt in the session, in particular what information sources they plan to use that they haven't been using to date. Send emails out to every student in the class just before their next assignment is due to remind them of what they put on this card, along with links to further help. *Looking forward to future learning.*

What can the library do for you?

Techniques used from this book: Bag of fears; I will do it; Library bingo.

Target audience: Staff you want to promote your library resources to, whether it is a health library, a commercial library such as a law library, a college or university library, or any other.

Maximum class size: Small, recommend around 12 per instructor at most, to allow one-to-one attention.

Expected outcomes: Learners will be able to:

- List the types of resources the library holds for their use.
- List the help the library can give them.
- Express the value the library can add to their activities.

Time: 30 minutes.

Handouts required: Set of generic handbooks or guides on how to use library resources.

Equipment required: Two pieces of A5/A6 card for each member of the class. Some small bars of chocolate or bags of sweets as prizes. Flip chart and paper.

Outline of session:

0–5 minutes: Introduction to session. Outline what will be covered in the session, including the expected outcomes. Explain why these outcomes will be important to them. *Introduction and setting the scene.*

6–10 minutes: Pass a piece of card to everyone attending the session. Ask them to write down the key things they'd like to learn from the day's session about the library. Collect these in to the front and quickly look through them during the next activity to group them according to theme. It is likely that some of the requested learning outcomes won't be covered in this session, so this activity lets you acknowledge that and summarise at the end of the session the sources of further help that would address these areas of need.

11–15 minutes: Pass another piece of card per person to the class. Give them one minute to write down a list of resources your library holds. Run through a (no doubt impressive!) list of resources you have in your library service. They should tick off items from their list as you mention them.

The first person to have ticked five off their list should shout bingo and get a small prize. Once you have finished describing the library resources, ask if anyone has an item that you have not mentioned. This may be something they'd expect the library to provide access to that you don't currently provide, so can give you a good insight into what your potential users expect from your service. Offer additional prizes to the people with the most items on their list. *Objective – list the types of resources the library holds for their use.*

16–20 minutes: Ask one person at a time to name a service (not resource) that the library offers, such as information skills teaching, inter-library loans, literature searching, etc. As you write each service down, ask for a show of hands on how many people were aware of that service. Fill in any gaps in the services that they are able to name at the end. *Objective – list the help the library can give them.*

21–25 minutes: This is your opportunity to say what a difference you make in providing the resources and services you've already discussed. For academic libraries, there is evidence linking library usage with academic achievement (dating back to the 1960s, for instance Kramer and Kramer (1968) or Barkey (1965)); for health libraries you are likely to be able to point towards the direct contribution you make to supporting evidence based practice and the policies of your institution; for libraries in commercial organisations you are likely to have collected evidence proving your impact. Whatever type of library your are in, spend five minutes describing this evidence and if appropriate give copies of this evidence to take away (for instance, journal articles describing the link between academic achievement and library usage). *Objective – express the value the library can add to their activities.*

26–30 minutes: Signpost places for help on using the library resources, making sure you cover the areas written on the cards used in the first activity. If several people have stated they want help with something in particular, you could at this stage announce a further session to be arranged in the near future to address that need. Ask everyone to tell you, one at a time, the way they think the library will be most useful to them in the future.

Bit of a strange session for assessment, in that very little assessment is clearly done during the session. The key assessment for this session is instead to think about if you made an impact. Do the attendees make greater use of the library and its resources afterwards? Think of ways you can assess this in your own library service.

References

Kramer, L. and Kramer, M. (1968) 'The college library and the drop-out', *College & Research Libraries*, 29 (4): 310–12.

Barkey, P. (1965) 'Patterns of student use of a college library', *College & Research Libraries*, 20 (2): 115–18.

Writing your literature review

Techniques used from this book: Model literature review; Buzz groups; I will do it.

Target audience: Anyone carrying out an extended project, part way through the process of gathering information for the literature review. Most relevant to higher education final year undergraduates and postgraduate students. Could also be adapted for lower levels where lots of information needs to be gathered from a range of sources.

Maximum class size: Small, perhaps up to 12 people.

Expected outcomes: Learners will be able to:

■ Evaluate the current state of their literature review and identify deficiencies.

■ Be aware of the range of materials available that they can use for their literature review.

■ Prepare an action plan for their continuing literature review.

Time: 60 minutes.

Handouts required: Any standard handouts you've previously used on accessing information, advanced search techniques, referencing or anything else you feel may potentially be useful.

Equipment required: A bucket of building blocks per table.

Outline of session:

0–5 minutes: Introduction to session. Outline what will be covered in the session, including the expected outcomes. Explain why these outcomes will be important to them. *Introduction and setting the scene.*

6–10 minutes: Split the class into small groups, each of which has a bucket of building blocks on their table. Ask the learners (individually) to construct the current state of their literature search in building blocks. *Objective – evaluate the current state of their literature review and identify deficiencies.*

11–20 minutes: When the models are made, ask them to explain their models to the whole class. If you are in a larger class you may need to ask them to explain to the members of their table rather than the whole class. Note down the problems that people list with their literature reviews –

you should find similar problems recurring regularly. For instance, several people may describe their models as 'spread out' or 'lacking focus' where they have struggled to narrow down their topic. Others may describe them as 'narrow' or 'tall' where they have found lots of material on a narrow topic, but have struggled to put it in the context of the wider literature. *Objective – evaluate the current state of their literature review and identify deficiencies.*

21–30 minutes: Display a list of information sources you feel may be useful to the subject areas being studied by the class. Run quickly through them one at a time, including what you feel they are most useful for. As you discuss each one, ask the class to vote whether or not they have been using the resource. *Objective – be aware of the range of materials available that they can use for their literature review.*

31–35 minutes: Quickly demonstrate the most underused resources, according to the votes received. *Objective – be aware of the range of materials available that they can use for their literature review.*

36–40 minutes: You should have an idea of the types of problems the people in the class are experiencing. Give each small group of students a problem to address. They have five minutes to list a few strategies to help sort that problem. *Objective – prepare an action plan for their continuing literature review.*

41–50 minutes: Ask each group to report to the class their strategies for solving the problem you gave them. When they have listed their solutions, open it up to a whole class discussion to add to the list of strategies. List these strategies at the front of the class for people to take notes from. *Objective – prepare an action plan for their continuing literature review.*

51–55 minutes: Ask each person in the class to think back to the model they made at the start of the session and imagine how they could turn it into their ideal literature review. They should then write down three things they intend doing differently when going back to their literature review in the near future. *Objective – prepare an action plan for their continuing literature review.*

56–60 minutes: Sum up some of the key themes of the session. Show them the handouts you have that may address some of the problems people identified and make them available to take as people leave the session. *Summarise the session.*

Further resources

There are a range of books available with useful tips for your teaching. The following are just a small selection that we feel may be particularly useful.

Bellanca, J. (2008) *200+ Active Learning Strategies and Projects for Engaging Students' Multiple Intelligences.* 2nd edn. Thousand Oaks, CA: Corwin Press.

Blanchett, H., Powis, C. and Webb, J. (2010) *A Guide to Teaching Information Literacy: 101 Tips.* London: Facet Publishing.

Eastwood, L., Coates, J., Dixon, L., Harvey, J., Ormondroyd, C. and Williamson, S. (2009) *A Toolkit for Creative Teaching in Post-Compulsory Education.* Maidenhead: Open University Press.

Gardner, H. (1983) *Frames of Mind: The Theory of Multiple Intelligences.* New York: Basic Books.

Ginnis, P. (2005) *The Teacher's Toolkit: Promoting Variety, Engagement, and Motivation in the Classroom.* Norwalk, CT: Crown House Pub. Co.

Harmin, M. and Toth, M. (2006) *Inspiring Active Learning: A Complete Handbook for Today's Teachers.* 2nd edn. Alexandria, VA: Association for Supervision and Curriculum Development.

Honey, P. and Mumford, A. (2000) *The Learning Styles Helper's Guide.* Maidenhead: Peter Honey Publications.

Powell, R. (1997) *Active Whole-Class Teaching.* Stafford: Robert Powell.

Secker, J., Boden, D. and Price, G. (2007) *The Information Literacy Cookbook: Ingredients, Recipes and Tips for Success.* Oxford: Chandos.

Silberman, M. (2005) *101 Ways to Make Training Active.* San Francisco, CA: Pfeiffer.

Smith, A. (1998) *Accelerated Learning in Practice: Brain-Based Methods for Accelerating Motivation and Achievement.* Stafford: Network Educational.

Tileston, D. (2007) *Teaching Strategies for Active Learning: Five Essentials for Your Teaching Plan.* Thousand Oaks, CA: Corwin Press.

Index